Boulevard of Dreams

CROATIANS AND EDUCATION IN ONTARIO

REVISED EDITION

ZORAN PEJOVIĆ, Ph.D.

CANADIAN SCHOLARS' PRESS   TORONTO

1994

Boulevard of Dreams: Croatians and Education in Ontario
Revised Edition

First published in 1994 by
Canadian Scholars' Press Inc.
180 Bloor St. W., Ste. 402,
Toronto, Ontario M5S 2V6

Copyright © Zoran Pejovic and Canadian Scholars' Press.
All Rights Reserved. No reproduction, copy or transmission
of this publication may be made without written permission.

Canadian Cataloguing in Publication Data

Pejovic, Zoran, 1955–
    Boulevard of dreams: Croatians and education in Ontario

Rev. ed.
Includes bibliographical references.
ISBN 1-55130-057-5

1. Croats – Education – Ontario. 2. Croatian
Canadians – Education – Ontario.* I. Title

LC3734.2.06P4   1994   371.97'91823071   C94-932606-2

Page layout by Brad Horning, Toronto

Printed and bound in Canada

For my sons
ANTHONY AND CHRISTOPHER

*Your names inked on this paper
are inimitable to the reality that they
are forever carved in my heart.*

Contents

Table of Contents		vii
List of Tables		ix
Foreword		xi
Acknowledgements		xv
Introduction		xvii
Chapter 1	EDUCATIONAL ASPIRATIONS: WHAT MATTERS?	3
	The Variables	4
	Socio-economic Origin	4
	Gender	9
	Ethnic Origin	12
	Religious Origin	20
	Regional Origin	21
	Peer Influence	24
	Parental Influence	26
	Self-concept	29
	Perception of Opportunity	32
	Summary	33
Chapter 2	EQUALITY OF OPPORTUNITY? PERCEPTIONS OF THE EDUCATIONAL SYSTEM	35
	Summary	53
Chapter 3	CROATIANS	55
	Croatia	55
	Croatians in Canada	58
	Summary	66

Chapter 4	STUDY METHODOLOGY	67
	The Sample	68
	Research Design	68
	Operationalization of Variables	69
	Data Analysis	74
	Summary	74
Chapter 5	RESULTS	75
	Tests of Hypotheses	75
	Summary	104
Chapter 6	DISCUSSION	107
	Socio-economic Origin Variables	107
	Demographic Variables	113
	School Variables	116
	Self-concept of Ability	117
	Summary	118
Chapter 7	CONCLUSIONS	119
	Limitations of the Study	119
	Conclusions	121
	REFERENCES	125

LIST OF TABLES

Table 1	Aspirations by Father's Education	76
Table 1A	Aspirations by Father's Education	77
Table 2	Aspirations by Mother's Education	78
Table 3	Aspirations by Father's Occupation	79
Table 3A	Aspirations by Father's Occupation	80
Table 4	Aspirations by Mother's Occupation	82
Table 5	Aspirations by Family Income	83
Table 6	Aspirations by Gender	85
Table 7	Aspirations by Grade Level	86
Table 8	Aspirations by Type of School	87
Table 9	Aspirations by Grades Received	88
Table 10	Aspirations by Ability Compared with Close Friends	89
Table 10A	Aspirations by Ability Compared with Close Friends	90
Table 11	Aspirations by Ability Compared with Classmates	92
Table 11A	Aspirations by Ability Compared with Classmates	93
Table 12	Aspirations by Ability to Graduate from University	94
Table 12A	Aspirations by Ability to Graduate from University	95
Table 13	Aspirations by Ability to Complete a Postgraduate Degree	96

Table 14	Aspirations by Country of Birth	97
Table 15	Aspirations by Place of Residence	98
Table 16	Aspirations by Numbers of Siblings	99
Table 17	Aspirations by Birth Order	100
Table 17A	Aspirations by Birth Order	101
Table 18	Multiple Regression of Aspirations by Family Income, Mother's Occupation, Father's Occupation, Father's Education, and Mother's Education	103
Table 19	Multiple Regression of Aspirations by Income, Mother's Education, Father's Occupation, Father's Education, Mother's Occupation, Gender, Ability Compared with Close Friends, Ability Compared with Classmates, Ability to Graduate from University, and Ability to Complete Postgraduate University	104
Table 20	Multiple Regression of Aspirations by Gender, Ability Compared with Close Friends, Ability Compared with Classmates, Ability to Graduate from University and Ability to Complete Postgraduate University	105

Foreword

Within academic writing the principal criterion of quality is the ability of the researcher to anticipate a conclusion in a new way, which "requires all sorts of complex instrumental, conceptual, and mathematical puzzles.... It is no criterion of goodness in a puzzle that its outcome be intrinsically interesting or important" (Kuhn, p. 36). It is therefore very refreshing to read a piece of academic work that is interesting, innovative, and, above all, a useful contribution to effective social intervention.

Ethnic cultural groups are unequal in their visibility to members of the cultural mainstream. These small groups are virtually invisible. In official statistics they are hidden under the heading "others" or a different generic name. Lack of specific information on vivid cultural specificity of these groups leads us to generalize about them. In the best case, our image of these ethnic groups is constructed by the base of our knowledge of sociological theory.

Pejović's work documents that such an approach may be misleading. There is nearly universal consensus that children who come from lower socio-economic status families have lower educational aspirations than children from middle- and upper-class homes. Pejović offers strong proof that this is not true for his sample of Croatian high school students in Toronto. No dimension of parental socio-economic status has a measurable effect on the educational aspirations of these students.

The fact that the strength of culture, even if imported in a new and by definition hostile, sociocultural environment may nullify the expected effects of postindustrial society is exciting from the point of view of sociological theory.

In the search for roots of deep respect for education within his ethnic group, Pejović offers a concise but deep insight into the history of Croatians at home and in Canada. This, in the context of the book, may give the reader a better understanding of the present dramatic changes in Croatia.

Equally seminal are Pejović's findings. Educators play an important role in the process of unofficial and invisible streaming, which exists in Canadian high schools. This task is very difficult, as the educator has to base his or her decision on incomplete information. Even a socially responsible and sensitive educator depends on "educated labelling," on application of generalized knowledge.

If motivation plays an important role in the process of post-secondary education, then for some cultural groups this type of generalization may lead to a sad waste of talent. Pejović documented this in the case of Croatian students. An educator on the basis of his or her experience and knowledge of social sciences may tend to predict a rather bleak educational future for ethnic students from a lower-class family whose parents have a rural background have and little or no education. This type of general education is intangible because of the cultural specificity of a small and relatively little-known cultural group.

Pejović's book may offer important knowledge to many in our educational system. It submits important information relevant for the creation of optimal strategies for students belonging to this specific ethnic group. More importantly, this book sensitizes the reader to the dangers of generalizations. Many rules, principles, and tools successfully used for the interpretation of mainstream society fail in their analysis of a subculture. The mechanical application of these standard interpretational procedures possesses all the negative attributes of an ethnocentric approach.

The methodology Pejović used in this book is clean, clever, and elegantly simple. The reader is able to follow the author's analysis step by step. Thus, this book may be inspirational reading for those who are entering the interesting world of sociological research. It is useful additional reading in courses of research methodology.

Pejović's work must be read not only by professionals in the realm of social sciences, but also by practitioners and, above of all, by the

FOREWORD

policy-makers. Findings in this book are significant for policy-making in the educational system. However, the awareness of differences among cultural groups and sensitivity toward these differences are important assets for any decision-makers operating within the political system of the Canadian mosaic. If at least some of them read and understand, Pejović's contribution to the improvement of the real lives of all of us is not negligible.

I sincerely hope that Pejović's writing will provoke readers to think once more about the position of education in the system of values of postindustrial society. If at least some readers think about the unquestioning and non-pragmatic admiration of education by members of an ethnic group whose culture is rooted mostly within a rural society and compare it with our increasingly utilitarian perception of education as utility, then the book will fulfill an important task.

Dr. Miroslav Disman

Associate Professor
Department of Sociology
York University
Toronto, Canada

Acknowledgements

It is with insurmountable gratitude that I salute the people who believed that an immigrant is capable of more than building bricks. Their encouragement was the catalyst in the completion of this study.

I would like to thank Mrs. Pina Pejović for her brilliant interpretation of what often became a statistical nightmare. Without you it could never be. You are the best!

I would like to thank my mother, Mrs. Vjekoslava Boba Sopta, for her encouragement and belief that her son is capable of producing a piece of work that does not necessarily fit the traditional mould of immigrant success. To my stepfather, Predrag Sopta, I extend sincere gratitude for his guidance and friendship.

I also acknowledge with appreciation Mr. Brad Lambertus and Ms. Helen Jager of Canadian Scholars' Press for their assistance in the preparation of this manuscript.

Finally, I would like to thank all the Croatian youth whom I encountered during my research, for without their cause this book would have remained only an idea.

Introduction

A modern industrial society, such as North America, offers a wide range of occupational opportunities, from those requiring several years of formal education to those that require only a limited amount of schooling. How individuals aspire to take advantage of these occupational opportunities is not based on some innate quality but is highly influenced by one's environment. In other words, individuals are, from birth, "socialized" to prevailing values in their own families and in society at large that affect their subsequent aspirations.

The socialization process begins with the first cries of the newborn child, a child that arrives into a society that is already loaded with biases that both the child and parents must face. But it is not simply a matter of absorbing. Society is differentiated, and the child grows up in a family that is located in one of the various levels of social status. As John Porter puts it, "there is the social inequality between children arising from the fact that early growth takes place, in the main, in the families with vastly different resources and values" (Porter et al., 1982:25). This difference in socialization will obviously have an effect on children's aspirations. These aspirations may be viewed as the "motivational prerequisites for filling a complex structure of adult roles, particularly those of the work world" (Porter et al., 1982:26).

The educational system at the primary and secondary levels must, as part of its mandate, assess and rank students' abilities, which will determine whether they go directly to work or whether they proceed to higher studies either in colleges, which will afford them specific skills, or universities, which for the most part will prepare them for professional careers.

One would hope that this assessment at the primary and secondary school levels would be based purely on ability. However, studies (Anisef et al., 1985; Clifton, 1982; Guppy, 1984; Higginbotham, 1985; Jansen, 1981; Rudd, 1984) have shown that variables such as ethnicity, gender, and socio-economic background play a very important role in shaping students' goals. These studies have shown that, regardless of one's intellectual ability, factors such as ethnic background, the socio-economic status of the family, and gender determine whether students aspire to or expect to attend post-secondary education.

Access to post-secondary education in Canada has, over time, been the focus of many learned debates. Sociologists (Acock, 1985; Calliste, 1980; Dimaggio and Mohr, 1985; Otto and Haller, 1977; Porter, Porter, and Blishen, 1982; Stafford, Lunstedt, and Lynn, 1984; and others) have proposed and tested variables they felt contributed to the formation of educational aspirations.

The focus of this study will be an examination of a select number of variables associated with educational aspirations. Specifically, it is the writer's intention to discover the effects that variables such as socio-economic origin, gender, ethnic origin, religious origin, regional origin, peer influence, parental influence, self-concept, and perception of opportunity have on the formation of educational aspirations among Croatian high school students in the Toronto area.

Boulevard of Dreams

**CROATIANS AND EDUCATION IN ONTARIO
REVISED EDITION**

CHAPTER ONE

Educational Aspirations: What Matters?

There have been many factors under study that are considered to be associated with educational aspirations. It will be conceptually useful to begin by presenting a clear definition of educational aspirations. The complexity that has accompanied the use of the term is partially due to the common practice of grouping educational aspirations and educational expectations together. Researchers have nevertheless attempted to define the terms in different ways. Williams (1972) chose to define "aspirations" as a "future state" that an individual desires to attain personally. On the other hand, he feels that expectations define a desire that the student's significant others have for his or her future status (1972:108). The focus of his study was a comparison between aspirations that the student may have for himself or herself as opposed to the expectations that the student's significant others, such as teachers, counsellors, and parents may hold.

Other distinctions between aspirations and expectations have been made that bear a closer resemblance to the model that this author wishes to adopt. Brookover (1967) and Sewell and Shah (1968) define educational aspirations as the goal that the student would like to attain, while expectations reflect the student's realistic choice of a goal. The general findings reported in the literature (Calliste, 1980; Howell and Frese, 1979; Porter, Porter, and Blishen, 1982; Rodman, 1967) indicate that one's aspirations are in general higher than one's expectations. Therefore, one's aspirations may be viewed as one's ideal attainment goals, while expectations would reflect one's realistic goals.

Recognizing the complexities of the literature covered, it is well to begin the present discussion with a review of the research pertaining to the investigation of select variables deemed as influential in the educational aspirations-formation process.

THE VARIABLES

Socio-economic Origin

Numerous studies (Anisef, 1985; Anisef, Paasche and Turrittin, 1980; Agnew, 1983; Breton, 1970; Kahl, 1953; Kerckhoff and Campbell, 1977; Porter, Porter and Blishen, 1973; 1982; Rosen, 1959) have demonstrated the importance of socio-economic origin in determining educational aspirations. Porter, Porter, and Blishen, in their study entitled "Does Money Matter," indicate that "all studies of what high school students hope and expect to do after high school show a relationship between their educational aspirations...and their social class position" (1973:42). They report that "this is such a well established finding, that if...a survey did not show such a relationship, the methodology of the survey would be suspect" (Porter, Porter, and Blishen, 1973:42). The importance of this variable has been maintained in numerous studies. Kahl (1953), in the pioneering work "Educational and Occupational Aspirations of 'Common Man' Boys" based on an interview sample of twenty-four high school males in the Boston area, found that while

> all had enough intelligence to go to college and thereby get a good start toward the higher levels of occupational life... one-half of the boys chose not to strive for such success. Instead, they planned little or no schooling beyond high school and said they would be content with lesser jobs that would likely be open to them (1953:186).

The study concludes with a proposal that argues that the most influential variable in optimizing the educational potential of "common man" boys was parental reinforcement. However, it is interesting to note the faith that working-class parents placed in the educational institution, particularly in its teachers. As one respondent's mother replied:

> I don't go to see the teachers. I figure the teachers know what they're doing. When I go up there I can't talk good enough. Some women go up there, and I don't know, they're so la-ti-ta. But I can't talk that way. Me, I'm just plain words of one syllable and that's all. The teachers, they'd just as soon not have you get into their way.... They know what they're doing (Kahl, 1953:195).

Furthermore, parents who wanted to succeed often pointed to their lack of education as a major handicap. Kahl elaborates: "rarely did they complain that the people who got ahead were the sons of bosses.... Instead they saw an occupational world stratified according to the basic principle of education" (Kahl, 1953:208). As such it may be inferred that these people felt that their occupational attainment depended solely on their level of education. Their socialization was instrumental in their acceptance of the dominant class's status quo.

Studies such as the one by Clark, Cook, and Fallis (1975) reached similar conclusions. They note that children who come from lower socio-economic status families lack an achievement orientation that children from middle- and upper-class families seem to possess. Indeed, as Kahl concluded, "most boys...from high status homes planned a college career, whereas most boys...from low status homes did not aspire to higher education" (1953:188).

Similar results in the relatively limited number of Canadian studies were found by Anisef, Paasche, and Turrittin (1980); Anisef et al. (1985); Calliste (1980); Porter, Porter, and Blishen (1982); Williams (1972). These studies provided sample evidence illustrating that lower-class students do not succeed educationally to the extent that middle- or upper-class students do. In a study on university access in British Columbia, Guppy (1984) reported that

> just under 90 per cent of the people born in this province will never get within spitting distance of a university or college... the spitting distance is furthest for children born in the homes of the working class. The probability of kids from working-class backgrounds going on to attain a university degree is

well below that for kids from upper-class backgrounds [in order of a 300 per cent difference]. And that probability has changed very little through time.... Despite increasing rhetoric concerning quality, over time the educational disparity, at the university level, between the working class and the upper class has diminished very, very little (Guppy, as quoted in Anisef et al., 1985:184).

This inequality of opportunity reflects the situation within the educational system of Ontario. Porter, Porter, and Blishen, surveying educational aspirations of high school students in Ontario, showed that inequality of opportunity in relation to aspirations was directly related to socio-economic status regardless of ability, attitude, or school performance (1973:105). In an updated study Porter, Porter, and Blishen, reported that "while 77 per cent of high mental ability boys of the upper middle class wanted to graduate from university, only 47 per cent of the lower class did." For the females in the sample the percentages were 61 and 36, respectively (1982:62). Therefore it seems that those who are disadvantaged the most by the system are children of working-class parents.

Porter, Porter, and Blishen further reported: "The rational model of an educational system...suggests that the most talented should be steered into the most intellectually demanding forms of education, if for no other reason than that the most complex tasks in the society requiring most education should be undertaken by the most able" (1982:63). The study continued: "The allocation of talent to training should be voluntary, and able children should be free...to choose whatever education they want.... But as we have seen, there are great differences between classes — so great, in fact to suggest that the Ontario system is not rational" (1982:63). Hence, working-class children can perceive the middle-class world, but they do not have the means or the capabilities of achieving status within this environment. Although they are taught the values prescribed by the middle-class environment, they often obtain the label of underachievers, thereby possibly precluding the opportunity for upward social mobility.

In Toronto, as Martell claims, the working-class parent is constantly aware that "the lower down the socio-economic scale you were, the fewer skills your kids had, the lower their track in school and the worse their job on graduation" (1974:19). This trend is once again illustrated by Porter et al. (1982) who point out that 18 per cent of high mental ability, lower-class males aspired towards college education. Only two per cent of the upper-middle-class, high mental ability cohorts chose college over work or university. Furthermore, 57 per cent of the grade 12 sample coming from the lower class wished to leave school after grade 12, while 24 per cent of the highest socio-economic class wished to do the same (1982:58-61).

The evidence indicates that the development of strong educational aspirations, expectations, and eventual attainment is most likely to be nurtured in the children of middle- and upper-class parents, while for children of lower-class parents it may be curtailed. Empirical evidence collected by Breton (1970) based on a sample of 150,000 Canadian high school students has shown that "70 per cent of the students from a high socio-ecnomic background expected to attend post-secondary institutions as against 59 per cent from a low socio-economic background" (Breton, as quoted by Calliste, 1980:14).

Temple and Polk (1986) presented findings of educational aspirations and attainment in a twelve-wave longitudinal study of students in Oregon. The first wave started in 1964 with 1227 high school sophomore males. The twelfth wave consisted of 240 individuals. The age range for the presented data was 16 to 31 years. The twelve waves of data represented the almost yearly sets of questionnaires that were distributed between 1964 and 1976 to the respondents. Thus, from combining the results of all the waves, aspiration data on 79 per cent of the sample were obtained. When they combined the effects of the most powerful variables on college aspirations (in their opinion these were family support and high school success), they found that the direct effect of socio-economic background was minimal. However, when they looked at it as an antecedent variable, they found that the effect, while indirect, was strong. In their view, socio-economic status "affects college plans through the family support and school success variables" (1986:82).

In terms of actual college entry they found that social class had a greater direct effect than family support. In a discriminant function equation, predicting entry into graduate school, social class once again became a very strong direct predictor (1986:83). While their study consisted of only a male cohort, thus showing some limitations, they rightfully concluded that:

> Static models can have considerable influence at one point in the educational attainment process but very little at other points. For example, the present findings suggest that social class has less influence on the formation of college plans and on college survival than on decisions to enter college and

graduate school. Any single measure of the importance of social class would average out this mix of negligible and positive contributions and underestimate what may be its key role at "particular points" in the educational attainment process (1986:84).

Anisef et al. (1985), commenting on the expansion of university access in Canada, proposed that this "educational expansion has not measurably reduced existing social class differentials" (1985:3). They expanded upon this statement, "a large proportion of individual differences in educational attainment are consistently accounted for by non-scholastic [social and cultural background] factors" (1985:4).

Consequently, it is argued that social background seems to be a very important indicator of both educational and occupational upward mobility. Indeed, as Larter and her colleagues in a study of post-secondary plans of grade 8 students in Toronto elaborated:

> The parents of the students in the affluent area, while giving the impression that they don't care what their children do so long as they are happy, do, nevertheless, exert tremendous pressure on their children to remain in the academic stream and follow a course that will one day lead to university (1982:52).

Moreover, they indicate that the parents of the children in

> the downtrodden area expressed little interest in their children getting a university education. In fact not one of the parents we talked to had the slightest idea what a university education entails. Furthermore, none of these parents perceived university as viable alternative in that it is so contrary to their everyday experiences. One father explained, what's the point of letting my son live in the dream world? Sooner or later he's gonna have to know what it means to make a buck (1982:52).

Accordingly, Larter et al. agree with a comment by Oakes who [on the leverage of educational system] implies that there is a "reduced willingness to devote educational resources to poor and ethnic minority children. It is on those at the top that economic hopes, and therefore educational resources, are pinned" (1986:71).

GENDER

In addition to class-based models, there is overwhelming evidence to indicate the significance of gender. It is clear that gender role patterns are distinct in most cultures, therefore it is reasonable to anticipate gender differences in relation to students' educational aspirations. Fleming (1974) found that, while controlling for variables such as socio-economic status, only two females for every five males had aspirations to attend university.

In a Canadian study carried out by Williams (1972) it was postulated that "educational attainments are seen as having considerable instrumental value for males, whereas for females such attainments are regarded as having limited instrumentality at best" (1972:113). In his equally represented sample of 3867 grade 12 students, he concluded that educational attainments for females are de-valued in general and particularly in lower socio-economic strata families "where material support for an extended education is limited" (1972:128).

Similar findings are once again described by Porter, Porter, and Blishen (1973). They postulated that in situations where there is limited family income, educational aspirations will definitely be gender related. Males are most likely to be encouraged to pursue their education, while females are more apt to be channelled in vocational directions. While these attitudes were most evident in working-class groups, they were also a prominent factor in cultural groups where clear male and female roles existed.

In an update of their work, Porter et al. (1982) suggested that "boys' education and occupation are closely related, and boys realize their ambitions and attain their status through their occupations. Girls are taught to realize their ambition through marriage, and to accept passively the social status which their husbands bring them" (1982:213). Furthermore, "women have a relatively lower opinion of their ability than men, and they maintain this low opinion despite evidence to the contrary, such as high grades at school" (1982:213).

Porter et al. subsequently contend:

> This low self-concept is in part a result of accepting the stereotyped image of the female as less able to cope intellectually and personally, and in part a result of subordinate roles which women see other women generally performing in the society. The truly "feminine" woman does not compete with men but takes a secondary position to them, silently

> acknowledging their greater ability and judgment. The process becomes self fulfilling. Women, thinking of themselves as less able, do not prepare themselves by obtaining further education or skills, and therefore they are, in fact, less able as adults to cope in various fields (1982:225).

One would believe that the educational system would strive to eradicate this socialization pattern. Instead, as the literature illustrates, males continue to be "directed by guidance branches of high school...to seek further training in order to obtain a better paying, more interesting job" (Porter et al., 1982:214). The authors explain:

> for girls, further training is very often seen (by guidance branches of high school...and by their parents) as a waste of time and money, since it is commonly thought that they will not use their skills for long [or even at all] in the work world. As mentioned above, despite the fact that the average woman leaving school today will spend twenty-five years of her life actively participating in the labour force, women are not encouraged or expected to improve their skills in order to upgrade their work potential (1982:215).

Hence, when students have aspirations that may contradict the traditional roles, it is likely that they will encounter negative support from a broad range of significant others. Pike (1977) alleges that most school teachers practice gender stereotyping. Thus, gender socialization of both male and female high school students is reinforced in the schools.

McIntyre (1975) commented on accessibility of Ontario universities to women:

> Two out of five undergraduate students are women. One in four graduate students is a woman. For every discipline dominated by women, three are dominated by men. In short, fewer women than men are entering university, fewer still are continuing on to graduate school and at both levels women are found in a limited number of what might be considered traditional fields (McIntyre as quoted by Anisef et al., 1985:101).

An empirical study by Calliste (1980) of the educational expectations of high school students in Ontario, based on a sample of 892 respondents, of which 519 were female, has shown that females have lower post-secondary expectations even when socio-economic background and ethnicity are controlled. Furthermore, females with high academic achievement have lower educational expectations than their male counterparts. She postulates that "the reason that fewer females than males expect to go to college or university [and expect to get high prestige jobs] is probably because it would be unrealistic for them to do so" (1980:225-226).

Calliste indicated that it is "both the structural barriers and childhood socialization processes [that] operate to limit females' occupational [educational] expectations" (1980:224). She described how "sex role socialization operates from infancy onward, first in the home and then in school, to channel females' aspirations towards the primary goal of marriage and the secondary goal of 'appropriate' feminine-dominated [and low prestige] occupations" (1980:225). Thus, the studies agree that

> independence is not encouraged in young girls by parents, girls do not develop self-confidence in their ability to cope with their environment. Since girls also receive less encouragement from parents to continue with their education [particularly lower-class girls whose parents maintain more traditional ideas concerning sex roles], and precisely because they have been reared to be overly dependent on the opinions of others, this lack of encouragement takes a high toll in terms of low aspirations (Porter et al., 1982:213).

Anisef et al. (1985) suggested that, as far as Ontario is concerned, a great deal of progress has been made. Utilizing data from the 1981 census, they have shown that "while university enrollment gaps between men and women [as a percentage of the 18–24-year-old population] was 6.6 per cent in 1961, the percentage in 1982 was only 2.6 per cent" (1985:102).

However, Porter et al. (1982) claimed that "when all institutions of post-secondary education in Ontario are examined, it is found that men constitute 61 per cent of the enrollment, women 38 per cent" (1982:213). Furthermore, they suggested that at the post-secondary, non-university, and undergraduate university levels, women are overrepresented in non-university institutions [community college]. Finally, 36 per cent of grade 12, high mental ability, low socio-economic status females aspired to graduate from university. For the males in the same category the figure was 47 per cent. For high mental ability, high socio-economic status, 61 per cent of females aspired to graduate from university, as did 77 per cent of the males in the same category (Porter et al., 1982:61).

Deosoran offers an interesting summary: "To be poor is bad enough, but to the extent university attendance is related to social privilege and nobility, to be poor and female is quite prohibitive" (1975:197).

ETHNIC ORIGIN

A third variable that may have been added to the above quotation and one that should be considered extensively in the literature on aspirations is ethnic origin. As Breton (1970) and Porter, Porter, and Blishen (1973) have pointed out, it seems that one's ethnic origin proves to be an excellent predictor of one's position on the vertical ladder of success.

One of the earlier works on the relationship between educational aspirations and ethnic origin was conducted in the United States by Rosen (1959) on a sample of 954 subjects. His sample consisted of six ethnic and racial groups, including French Canadians, Greeks, East European Jews, Southern Italians, Blacks, and the native-born Protestant group. Studying achievement motivation, value orientations, and educational vocational aspiration levels; Rosen postulated that Protestants, Jews, and Greeks have much higher achievement motivation than French Canadians, Blacks, and Italians. Further analysis illustrated that Jews, Protestants, and Greeks possess higher educational and vocational aspirations.

Although Rosen's above-mentioned study of "value orientation" and "motivation" has been disputed as explanations for ethnic achievement differences (Breton and Roseborough, 1971; Featherman, 1971; Li, 1978; Stryker, 1981), there are, nevertheless, certain trends that still reflect Rosen's findings. King (1968), in an archival study of data drawn from the Carnegie Human Resources Data Bank, which lists virtually all secondary school students in Ontario who attended school between 1959 and 1966, found that Jewish students continually had superior teacher ratings on the basis of achievement in school. He went on to state that "the performance of the groups [Jews] was so superior to that of other groups [Hungarian, German, Slovak, Ukrainian, Polish, and Italian] that no explanation could be found for it in terms of performance on standardized tests or disproportional representation in socio-economic groups associated with school success" (King, 1968:90).

Featherman replicated King's findings in a study of achievement of a number of religio-ethnic groups in the United States. He reported that the Jewish students in his sample "attain more years of schooling, higher levels of occupational prestige, and greater salaries and wages than all other subgroups" (1971:211). On the other end of the scale, Featherman claimed that those of Latin American and Italian origin had the lowest levels of achievement.

This variance of status among ethnic groups has been examined in a number of Canadian studies (Anisef, 1975; Anisef, et al., 1985; Clifton, 1982; Jansen, 1981; Li, 1988; Porter, 1965; 1976; 1979; Richmond, 1986; Clifton et al., 1986). All these studies reported differences in educational and occupational attainment among these various groups.

Porter (1965) postulated that ethnicity was a very important factor in the formation of the class system in Canada. In a study based on a number of census reports, it was shown that people of British origin were continually overrepresented in higher status occupational positions, while lower status positions were mostly occupied by those of Italian extraction.

This status inequality, based on ethnic background, is not the result of what Rosen (1959) termed the "achievement motivation-value orientation" syndrome, but rather it reflects the notion of what Li (1988) terms the "differential opportunity structure" inherent in the Canadian occupational and educational system. In his study on the stratification of immigrants in Toronto (based on the information gathered from the 1971 census), Li concludes that occupational status differentials among certain ethnic groups persist, even when one allows for such variables as education, social origin, and prior achieved occupational status.

Li claims that the British enjoy the highest status in the occupational structure, while the lowest occupational status is held by Poles and Italians. Concurring with the notion that the immigrants' educational level and prior occupational status is an important stratifying determinant, Li nevertheless concluded that "to the extent that immigrants with similar educational backgrounds and previous occupational levels are differentially stratified in the occupational structure on the basis of ethnic origin, one may claim the existence of discrimination" (Li, 1988:39). While Richmond and Kalbach (1980) disputes the findings, he still admits that certain ethnic groups (Jews) are overrepresented in post-secondary institutions when all other variables are held constant. Furthermore, as Breton and Rosenborough (1971), Featherman (1971), and Li (1978) conclude, motivational differences within these groups are insignificant factors in this ranking process.

Although Li's study deals with occupational stratification, one can certainly deduce the negative influences that such findings may have in cultivating educational aspirations within the disadvantaged ethnic groups. Furthermore, Li (1988) disputes Darroch's (1984) argument that in some contexts ethnicity disappears as an independent variable once factors such as class are held constant.

In essence, what the previous argument helps to illustrate is that there is a limited opportunity structure operating on the disadvantaged ethnic groups. If a student of Italian, Polish, or Hungarian extraction is continually socialized into perceiving the limitations to educational and occupational attainment potential simply based on his or her background, then one cannot dispute that this student may become fatalistic towards his or her chances of upward mobility.

Furthermore, chances for intergenerational upward vertical mobility (movement between the level occupied by parents and that occupied by their children) may seldom occur since, as Haller concludes, "people adjust their levels of aspiration so that they are usually not totally out of line with the prospects of attaining them" (1968:485).

Perhaps the issue that emerges herein and remains prevalent within many disadvantaged ethnic groups is the inferiority complex of these collectives. This complex may have been entrenched in the North American climate of the 1950s. In the United States they were considered the "unmeltable ethics." Kromkowski (1986), commenting on the United States' immigration policy from the early 1920s to the mid-1960s states that "a national immigration policy of selection and restriction effectively excluded immigrants from these regions of Europe using flawed social scientific rationales that tagged Eastern and Southern Europeans as undesirable and inferior" (1986:57).

In Canada, immigrants had to live within a dominant ideology best illustrated in the works of Stephen Leacock, professor of economics and a humourist, who, reflecting on the immigration policies of his time, commented "that as far as East Europeans [and others who were not of white, British Commonwealth stock] were concerned...a little dose of them may even by variation do good, like a minute dose of poison in a medicine" (Leacock as quoted in Porter, 1979:34).

In the 1950s and 60s, swelled by the new wave of immigration, these groups were still working to fit into what some have called the mould of Anglo conformity. Usually, limited in some instances by a failure to master the English language and ignorant of the host country's way of life, these groups may not enforce a sufficient degree of pressure in relation to their children's optimum educational attainment. As a demographic example, Anisef (1975) offers the case of the Italians.

A study by Anisef (1975) on the effects of ethnicity on occupational and educational aspirations Ontario grade 12 students showed that Italians had lower expectations than other ethnic groups. Although he proposed that these students aspired towards post-secondary education, they did not expect to enter it. Consequently, Jansen (1981), analyzing the educational attainment of Italians in Vancouver, showed them to be in the second lowest position, one higher than Native people. Jansen elaborates:

> Beyond compulsory school age or the secondary level of education, compared to other groups, Italians tend to be underrepresented. Various explanations are offered for this situation, including a lack of interest by the part of parents or a lack of interest by the group as a whole in higher education (1981:57).

Richmond (1986), in his study "Ethnogenerational Variation in Educational Achievement," comments that in Canada by 1981, according to the census of the same year, 63.6 per cent of the 25–44-year-old cohort possessed some sort of a diploma, degree, or certificate. He elaborates: "this average was exceeded by all immigrant birthplaces except the European aggregate" (1986:2). He further argues that Italians who came to this country as children were in a much better educational position than their parents. Indeed, he shows that their educational profile was much closer to the national average.

What Richmond is seemingly suggesting is that children of Italian immigrants are not suffering the perceived educational obstacles optimizing their educational potential. However, while some intergenerational mobility is evident, Richmond does not illustrate the extent of this progression past the compulsory school age. In other words, it may be possible that the intergenerational mobility is simply the result of compulsory educational attendance differentials between the two countries. Throughout most of Italy, children are required to attend school up to grade 8; in Canada, children must attend school until their sixteenth birthday, approximately grade 11.

A generalized attempt at illustrating the educational aspirations of Southeastern Europeans was carried out in a number of historiographical studies. Smith, as quoted by Bodnar, pointed out that, traditionally, "newcomers from Southern and Eastern Europe displayed a passionate and intensified concern for schooling in America" (1971:1). Reflecting the period between 1880 and 1930 he held that European Slavs, Rumanians, Greeks, and Jews aspired to the American dream of advancement through schooling (1971:1). However, he does not offer a clear picture of the divergent patterns of success that these groups set for themselves.

Ethnic differences in educational aspirations among Southeastern Europeans, and especially among Slavic collectivities, were engraved in the immigrant experience in the early 1990s. The prevailing notion at the time was that although education had a specific function, its function was, as Bodnar (1976) points out, unrelated to social advancement. Seemingly, the only type of educational aspirations immigrant children envisioned were the ones that contributed to "retaining the cultural, linguistic, and religious values of the ethnic group" (Bodnar, 1975:1).

This philosophy appears to have surfaced in the immigrant literature and was passed on to the second generation. Bodnar further postulates that language loyalty and religion were so important to the Slavic collective that, if the children attended schools where they did not receive native language instruction and religion, they were considered lost to that collective.

If a child were to have higher educational aspirations, such aspirations received approval from the community only if the education led to priesthood; otherwise young people were geared towards skilled trades. Perhaps it was this type of philosophy that led Rosen (1959) to explain the "achievement syndrome" by suggesting that ethnic groups with Roman Catholic affiliation moved up less rapidly than non-Catholic groups.

In viewing such patterns, one has to take into account the orthodox social climate in North America at that time. Certainly, Weber's Protestant "work ethic" dominated the social climate. His description of "personality types" was a replica of the person with high achievement motivation. Rosen (1959) concluded that Protestant-oriented collectives encouraged their children to develop high aspirations and set high goals.

Ultimately, Slavs may have been troubled by what they perceived to be materialistic greed exercised by the middle-class American values. They seemed reluctant to embrace the fast-moving, urban industrial society (Bodnar, 1976).

Breton elaborates:

much of the new immigration was from national ethnic groups whose cultures and primordial identities were suppressed by the great multinational empires of the times, the Russian and the Austro-Hungarian, and, that for many of the immigrants, their hopes were to save or revive their cultures in the New World. They may have chosen American freedom, seen not so much as the freedom of individual rights, but as collective rights for groups to be able to live their own cultural life away from oppression (Breton, 1970:146).

The children of these immigrants did not fare any better. Certainly, they did not seem to benefit from parental support when it came to developing high educational aspirations. Instead they were influenced by their parents to value immediate employment above lengthy education. As Bodnar described, "slavic parents held definite ideas, which influenced the educational prospects of their children drastically" (1975:5).

Among working-class families, parents did not encourage schooling. Rather, at the first opportune moment, they encouraged their children to enter the labour force and contribute to family survival. Bodnar reports that in a sample of Polish working-class families in Scranton, Pennsylvania during the 1920s, it was found that 35 per cent of family income was provided by school-age children (1975:6). He further reports that "Slavic parents routinely falsified working permits so that their children could begin work at 14 instead of the legal age of 16" (1975:5). If children rebelled by continuing their education, they were made to believe that it was more important to learn a manual skill than to attend school. In other words, if one learned a trade, one never went hungry.

Although this Slavic perspective was common to Bodnar's study covering the period between 1890 and 1940, it should be noted that there were Slavs, predominantly Slovenes, Czechs, and Poles from Germany, who emigrated from urban-based, industrially advanced parts of Europe and whose educational attainments and aspirations were similar to those of highy aspiring North Americans. These groups were usually perceived as socialists who valued philosophy and education far above religion and honest hard work. When in the 1930s they tried to advocate education as not only necessary for economic success but also as the only means to help stamp out worker exploitation, they were met by strong criticism from the church and other religious-based organizations (Bodnar, 1976:9-11).

In general, Slavs were strongly skeptical of education because they felt that it had little to offer to their particular needs and goals. Largely peasant-based, they were channelled into industry where they were preoccupied with worrying about daily living. As Bodnar's succinct and extremely well-researched study concludes, "this emerging working-class pragmatism reinforced elements of traditional peasant culture, such concerns with survival, limited visions of the future, and spiritual rather than material ends" (Bodnar, 1976:14).

This strong value internalization was not eliminated by the Slavs living in the United States and Canada in the 1950s. Although some of them were exposed to higher education as the ultimate means of mobility, they constantly failed as the majority were socialized into the attitudes of their parents.

The extent to which the Slavic philosophy concerning education failed to change in the 1960s and 1970s is perhaps hinted at in Radecki's (1979) study on Polish collectivity in Canada. He illustrates that in 1961 approximately 70 per cent of the Polish workforce in Toronto was represented in blue-collar occupations (1979:18). In a broader sample of the total Polish-Canadian workforce across Canada, similar results were found. Porter states that in the 1960s East Europeans were "overrepresented in agriculture as they have always been in Canada" (1979:52).

Based on the offered statistics, Radecki does not deal with the issues of educational aspirations among Poles. Subsequently, one cannot help but wonder to what extent the low educational aspirations of their forefathers were still ingrained in Poles living in Canada in the 1960s.

In the United States, the figures for Eastern European groups reflect the notion that occupationally they were still overrepresented in the manufacturing sector. Kromkowski (1986) offered results from an American census. The groups with the greatest representation within this sector, of the foreign-born cohort that arrived after 1965, were Polish, 45.9 per cent; Yugoslavian (all nationalities), 41.9 per cent; Bulgarians, 35.5 per cent; and Hungarians, 31.1 per cent. (1986:71).

Stafford et al., in "Social and Economic Factors Affecting Participation in Higher Education," suggest that for a large number of manufacturing jobs a college education is not needed. Hence, "if the percentage of the population employed in manufacturing is high, participation in higher education may be expected to be lower" (1984:597). The results demonstrate that these and other similar groups are educationally disadvantaged.

Nevertheless, studies of educational aspirations, in Canada and the United States, offer ample evidence that these groups have high aspirations. Porter et al. (1982), in a Canadian study of high school youth, proposed that of the Eastern European aggregate, 54 per cent aspired to go to university. However, in view of the recent demographic evidence, the question that remains to be answered is to what extent are these aspirations translated into attainment?

Burke, in "Educational Implications of Cultural Diversity," comments, "there are usually no special barriers to initial entry to elementary school, [but] subsequent entry to secondary and post-secondary institutions poses problems for cultural minorities" (1984:8). An article appearing in the *Toronto Star* the same year offers a pragmatic illustration. Entitled, "Schools Discourage Portuguese Students Parents' Group," the article attacks the local school system with blatant prejudice to Portuguese students in particular:

> Elementary school children who don't speak English as their first language are steered away from academic courses by Toronto's education system.... These students — considered "problems" from an early age — don't get the encouragement they need to stay in school.... they are assessed at an early age, before they can even speak English, put into special education programs, and saddled with that label for the rest of their academic years (1984, Nov. 28:A6).

Another article appearing in the same newspaper a year later illustrates similar concerns. The article points out that "too many Black students are pushed into basic and vocational high school programs.... This problem affects not just Blacks but East Asians, Italians, Portuguese, and Native Canadians" (*Toronto Star*, 1985, May 1: A6).

Additionally, an article commenting on the trends of education of immigrant children states that "teachers have often misjudged the potential of immigrant children and thus wrongly channelled them to vocational schools" (*Toronto Star*, 1987, March 2:A6).

Furthermore, Burke's "entry concept" may be curtailed by recent university trends that are making access generally more difficult. As an article appearing in the *Toronto Star* illustrates: "By forcing universities to tighten standards you exclude a disproportionate number of immigrant children, yet many of these children blossom in university, if only given a chance" (1984, Aug. 27:A8).

At this point the reader should take into consideration the fact that "ethnic origin" itself (in this section presented as a category) should not be viewed as a deterrent to high aspirations. Rather, ethnic origin has traditionally been linked to the formation of a related stereotype. As Jansen points out (personal communication), it is the stereotypes that consciously or unconsciously categorize the children of these groups into different educational streams.

RELIGIOUS ORIGIN

A number of studies (Featherman, 1971; Mueller, 1980; Stryker, 1981) documented a relationship between religion and educational aspirations. Earlier work by Rosen (1959) implied that Roman Catholics had lower educational aspirations than Protestants, in essence remarking on their negative view of intellectualism and upward social mobility. Featherman, in a study of five religio-ethnic groups in seven major cities in the United States, reports that Jews have high educational and occupational aspirations regardless of ethnic ancestry; at the same time, Roman Catholics of Mexican and Italian background have the lowest aspirations (1971:207).

Mueller (1980), in a study based on nine religious groups in the United States, proposed that the religion according to which an individual was raised has a significant influence on educational attainment. Nevertheless, its effects are minimal and should not be singled out in "discourses invoking religious achievement subculture" (1980:150). Interestingly, this is the first study that shows some Catholic groups exceed the educational attainments of some Protestant groups even when class status is taken into consideration.

A study by Stryker (1981) examines the effect of religion on the educational and occupational attainments of a group of Wisconsin secondary school students. Replicating Mueller's (1980) findings, Stryker discovers that religion has a minimal net effect on educational and occupational attainment. Occupational success is much more influenced by the respondent's ability and socio-economic status.

Porter et al. (1982) echo the findings in a Canadian study. When looking at the educational aspirations of students from a number of religious groups, they argue that there are no major differences in the aspirations of Catholics and major Protestant groups. This difference was particularly minimal in the grade 8 cohort where, as the authors propose, religious values are considered to be the strongest. Once again, the exception was the Jewish students who, in the grade 12 cohort, provided results showing that 75 per cent of the males and 62 per cent of the females aspired to attend university. For the grade 12 Protestant-Catholic cohort, the results showed 38 per cent of Catholics versus 44 per cent of Protestants aspired to attend university (1982:72-74). The authors conclude:

> The evidence indicates that for boys, in particular, there is little difference between Catholics and Protestants with respect to educaitonal aspirations.... We find little, that is, to substantiate the view that religious beliefs and values in themselves might be the source of differences in educational attainment and experience (1982:74-75).

REGIONAL ORIGIN

Regional origin, regional proximity, geographical location, and rural and urban settings are variables that researchers (Anisef et al., 1985) have found to be effective in the formation of educational aspirations. Anisef, Paasche, and Turrittin report that there is a great deal of hardship faced by a student from a rural background who is attempting to gain access to a post-secondary institution: "fewer high status students in the academic programs in the ...rural areas went on to university than did youth from more urban areas" (1980:24). The authors postulate that the:

> lower SES characteristics of rural areas, and their distance from post-secondary institutions posed a double hardship to students seeking access to higher educaiton...findings showed that the proportion of young people with post-secondary education experience varied strongly within the province (Ontario): 74 per cent in Toronto, 67 per cent in other large and small cities, and 52 per cent in towns and smaller rural areas (1980; 1985:104).

Porter et al. eloquently summarize:

> The rural way of life is probably not completely obliterated in present-day Ontario, particularly for communities farther from the major urban centres. Here, orientations to life can probably still be affected by the special relationships with

> nature, its mysteries and its rhythms, its hazards and its bounties, all of which could be the source of cultural and psychological characteristics quite different from those of the dweller in the megapolis (1982:65).

The fact that rural youth are not as exposed as their urban counterparts to a variety of occupations may, the authors propose, account for the differentiation in the formation of educational aspirations. Predominantly, rural youth are overrepresented in agricultural labour, a job that does not require high levels of education. Consequently, the authors elaborate:

> The farm population has been the least educated of any segment of society. The parental generation of present-day rural young people have low levels of educaiotn. They were brought up when the prevailing attitude was that a boy would become productive on the farm in relation to the growth of his physical strength, rather than his intellect. Thus the farmer saw schooling for his children as having limited use (1982:65).

As far as the differences in aspirations between rural and urban youth are concerned, the authors found that 25 per cent of rural males and 28 per cent of rural females wanted to graduate from university. For their urban counterparts the figures were 40 and 34 per cent respectively (1982:66-67). Guppy et al., studying changes in the patterns of education in Canada, based on a 1973 Canadian mobility survey cohort, point out that "for respondents from farming backgrounds, the [high school] completion rate is 36.2 per cent" (1984:322). Interestingly, the rate for respondents from managerial and professional families was 78.9 per cent. For the current cohort, the rates for high school completion among respondents from farming backgrounds increased to 58.8 per cent. The authors suggest this change is quite progressive (1984:322).

Still Porter et al. (1982) postulate that there is a relationship between educational aspirations and the degree of urbanization. Furthermore, "the [educational] horizons of those from rural areas are even more limited than those from urban surroundings" (1982:67).

Anisef et al. comment on regional disparity in university access across Canada:

> Access issues are strongly associated with a province's...urban development. In the more rural provinces such as Saskatchewan and Manitoba educational researchers and government consider geographical location a key variable in exploring accessibility.... The Atlantic provinces, suffering from high unemployment and poor economic outlook, have focused on the problems of getting traditional, non-urban males into urban-oriented, post-secondary institutions (1986:211).

As far as British Columbia is concerned similar results are found. Anisef et al. state that "differences between various regions within the province are great not only in terms of participation rates in higher educational institutions, but also in the type of program and institution chosen" (1986:186). They add:

> ...while 33 per cent of those who completed grade 11 in the North and West Vancouver area continued after grade 12 at a university or academic college program in 1972, the corresponding percentage for those from the Prince Rupert to Dawson Creek area was less than 13 per cent (1986:187).

Similar results in a 1980 study show that "some 25 per cent fewer grade 12 students from the non-metro [Toronto] region go on to university...about five metro students become full-time university students for every two from the non-metro group" (Anisef et al., 1986:187).

The situation in Quebec tends to view regional proximity not only from the point of urban-rural shift but also from the point of view that divides the regions into economically advantaged and disadvantaged regions. As such it seems that "students from privileged regions always have higher academic aspirations than students from disadvantaged regions" (Anisef et al., 1986:149).

The literature suggests that "origin variables" such as gender, socio-economic origin, ethnic origin, religious origin, and regional origin are significant factors in determining an individual's range of educational aspirations and expectations. However, in light of the vast amount of research, one must also consider other factors that may be deemed as instrumental in explaining the complexity of the development of educational aspirations.

PEER INFLUENCE

The literature indicates that peer influence may be added to the list of factors influencing educational-vocational aspirations and expectations. Research of this nature (Anisef et al., 1985; Cohen, 1983; Coleman, 1961; James, 1986; McDill et al., 1965; Otto, 1977; Picou and Carter, 1976; Reitzes and Mutran, 1980) has shown a positive relationship between peer influence and educational and vocational aspirations. Cohen (1983), while offering a critique, illustrates the consensus of the findings: "the size of the peer influence effect has been represented by the coefficient of direct path from best friend's college plans to respondent's college plans; coefficients for this path have often exceeded .2, suggesting a fairly substantial effect" (1983:728).

Herriott (1963), in a study of Massachusetts high school students' educational aspirations, found that those students who had a "friend the same age" as themselves had the same perceived aspirations as the friend. Kandel and Lesser (1969), in a study of secondary three schools' populations in the United States, extended Herriott's position by suggesting that influence of peers increases with the intimacy of the friendship.

This intimacy of friendship was further examined by Otto (1977), who singled out the influence of one's girlfriend and best friend on career achievement and aspirations. Otto's analysis was based on a 15-year follow-up study of 442 17-year-old male respondents in a number of Michigan high schools. He proposed that the strongest influence on educational attainment was wielded by girlfriends. He elaborates that

> Girlfriends are a specific form of peer relationship and share in the social network, which is most influential during the years when a youth is coordinating his educational, occupational, and marital plans. Her interests are intimately associated with his plans and her encouragement is likely to affect his career decisions (1977:287).

As Otto points out, increased involvement in a male-female personal relationship leads to an increase in isolation from others and, as such, the influence of a girlfriend becomes even more important. Although the study depends heavily on the memory of the respondents, thus exhibiting some weaknesses, and deals with educational attainments and career decisions, one can, nevertheless, see the parallel relationship to the girlfriend's influence on the male adolescent's educational aspirations.

In view of the above studies, it is imperative to note that students, especially those in adolescence, seek the approval of their peers concerning things that are important to their functioning. This period itself is usually characterised by traumas or as Berger (1972) elaborates, "[it is] ridden with conflict and tensions stemming partly from... the age-grading norms of our society that withhold from adolescents most of the opportunities, rights, and responsibilities of adults" (1972:54). Generally, the adolescent may be going through a period commonly referred to as an "identity crisis."

Thus, Pavalko and Bishop (1966) postulate that adolescents depend on communication with significant others for consensual validation. Picou and Carter offer a set of structural conditions that are conducive to the development of educational aspirations: "peer groups that are relatively small, homogeneous in make up, and isolated from other reference groups have a significant impact on the formation of educational and occupational aspirations" (1976:13).

Some of the studies (Kandel and Lesser, 1969) pertaining to the influences of peers are not specific in their explanation of how friends were selected or what the cultural backgrounds of the respondents were. Furthermore, in some instances there was a lack of information regarding the sex of significant others.

Some studies (Porter et al., 1982) suggest that there is a negative relationship between peer influence and university aspirations regardless of what controls are used" (1:47). They write: "It may be that students who are caught up in school social activities, or otherwise involved with peers...are less likely to have high educational aspirations" (1982:148). Cohen (1984) postulates that studies using path analysis tend to overemphasize the strength of the peer influence variable as a strong educational aspiration-formation predictor. He suggests that the discrepancy lies in the fact that the above studies do not account for intervening variables such as "initial similarity at the time of friendship selection and peer influence following friendship formation. Without controls for initial similarity the portion of eventual similarity due to influence is overestimated" (1984:728).

Hence, as James (1980) claims, students in many instances tend to associate with students who are similar to themselves. As such, this will likely influence the adolescent's decision in choosing to take a vocational, college, or university route.

PARENTAL INFLUENCE

Another factor shown by researchers to be related to educational aspirations is that of parental influence, or as Danziger (1975) classified it, "familialism." Porter et al. (1982) propose that

> parental influence is paramount in educational plans and aspirations. One of the ways in which it is felt by students is through the assistance and encouragement parents give regarding schoolwork. There is much evidence that such parental involvement has positive effects on aspirations (1982:149).

They state that "upper-middle-class boys and girls were much more likely than lower-class boys and girls to receive the assistance and encouragement that helps them to be academically successful" (1982:151). Consequently,

> middle- and upper-class boys were much more likely than those of the lower class to receive help from their parents.... the lower class mother played a more important role than did the father, in contrast to the upper-middle class where the father was more likely to help; [finally], there was a sizeable proportion of lower-class mothers who reported their children received no help from the family (1982:151-152).

Acock writes:

> Parents and children alone share a common location in the social structure. The occupational goals and motivations of adolescents may reflect the socio-economic status of their family instead of deliberate efforts of their parents. A teenager raised in poverty is far less likely to aspire to a high occupational status than the son or daughter of a surgeon (1985:165).

Sandis, in a 1970 study based on a sample of 254 New Jersey secondary school students and their mothers, claimed that "there is a positive asssociation between mothers' educational plans for their children and the students' own plans" (1970:219). Baker and Enwistle, in a study based on a sample of 1161 youngsters attending two schools — a white, middle-class suburban school and an urban-based, integrated school — in Baltimore, state that

> the mother's view of the school and the interpretation she places on events that occur in school could have many implications for children as they begin to fashion an academic self-image. For example, mothers can describe school to the child as a place where individuals have little room for self-direction or as a place where it pays to take some initiative (1987:671).

They conclude that there is a relationship between early socialization patterns that mothers confer on their children and educational aspirations. Particularly, young males are socialized into success-oriented traditional disciplines. Consequently, they concur with the belief that Levine (1976) held: "...U.S. parents held lower educational aspirations for daughters than for sons" (1987:672). Porter et al., reporting on the results of their study in Ontario, show that the "...overwhelming majority of parents, of boys particularly, wanted their children to go to university" (1982:180).

Acock, in a paper entitled, "Parents and Their Children: The Study of Intergenerational Influence," indicate that the mother is "the most influential parent.... This dominance on the part of the mother extends to instrumental areas...[such as]... work ethic" (1986:1612).

A study by Baker (1981), based on a sample of families with children 21 years of age or older, not living at home, in the midwestern United States, offers an analysis of the effect of dual employment families on educational attainment. While her study is based on attainment, parallels may be drawn to suggest the effects of dual employment on aspirations. Baker elaborates that the "mother's occupational status had a more powerful effect than father's on sons' attainment, while having an equal or less powerful effect... on daughters' attainment" (1981:251). The interesting point that this study made is that the mother's occupation, (which has traditionally been left out in studies dealing with "family dynamics" factors) proves to be a very important determinant of educational attainment and aspirations.

In general terms one may postulate, as Rehberg and Westby have so succinctly done, that "parents who are better educated, who hold the more prestigious occupations, i.e. those who are in the middle or upper social strata, generally display more positive values towards education, achievement and social mobility, and usually set higher career goals for their children" (1967:371). The study further shows that there is a negative relationship between family size and educational aspirations. Porter et al. (1973) echo these findings in a Canadian sample. Furthermore, the same results were obtained when they controlled for socio-economic background. In their study of aspirations of Ontario grade 12 students, Porter et al. concur that both birth order and number of children in the family have an effect on aspiration-formation:

> Whatever the class position, the more children there are in the family the greater the cost of keeping them out of the labour force and in school and university. With birth order, particularly if families are large, two possibilities exist: one is that educational resources might be expended on educating the older children; the other is that the younger children will benefit from a large number of income earners in the family (1982:84).

The authors conclude:

> Around 60 per cent of upper-middle-class children in small families of one or two children had (university) aspirations, compared to only 43 per cent of those in large families of five children or more. For middle-class families the corresponding difference in aspirations was 55 and 34 per cent, and for the lower class it was 35 and 17 per cent (1982:84).

Alwin and Thorton (1984), in "Family Origins and the Schooling Process" based on data from an 18-year longitudinal study of children and their families in the United States, concur with the general trends in the literature:

> The size of the family into which a person is born, as well as the growth in the size of the family, generate independent disadvantaging effects on the length of school attendance.... Social policies aimed at making need-based financial aid

available for college attendance, as a way of equalizing opportunity, have not removed the financial pressures suffered by larger families. Although financial need, which is presumably correlated with family size, is used as a criterion for allocating financial assistance to college matriculants, there appears to be an effect of family size which ultimately disadvantages persons from larger families (1984:799).

Concurrently, as quoted in Stafford et al. (1984):

> The influence which the circumstances of the parents have on their aspirations for the education of their children is clearly seen when we compare parents from different walks of life... rising educational attainments of parents will result in increasing aspirations for their children.... Those parents who did not themselves go beyond grammar school say they expect one out of three of their children to go to college, but those parents who themselves graduated from college expect all of their children to go to college (1984:606).

The authors agree with the general trends in the literature; there is a relationship between parental educational achievement, family size, and the level of children's aspirations.

SELF-CONCEPT

The literature has also shown the importance of self-perception or self-concept as a variable in the educational aspiration-formation process of young adolescents. The development of self-concept, however, starts with the earliest socialization trends. In particular, self-concept develops in the child's continued interaction with first his or her primary socializing agents, i.e., parents and consequently, secondary socializing agents such as peers, teachers, etc. This gradual process where the child learns through taking the role of the others reflects what Cooley called the looking-glass self. Hence,

> the child's self-concept is a reflection of the evaluation which others have built up of him in the varied contexts of socialization. Self-concept is affected, too, by structural factors:

the size of the family, the birth order of the child, the size of the community, socio-economic status of the family, and religious and ethnic affiliation. The children of minorities or workers in depressed single-industry towns, for example, learn to perceive themselves as they are seen by dominant majorities or middle-class professionals, including those of the educational system (Porter et al., 1982:27).

According to Calliste, "the self-concept is that organization of qualities the individual attributes to himself or herself" (1980:25). Expanding on this notion she postulates that these qualities may include the actor's ambition and intelligence as well as future role fulfillment. In other words, does the actor feel capable of fulfilling the role of a lawyer or a sanitary engineer? Wilson and Portes embellish: "A person develops and adjusts his aspirations in accordance with both the evaluations he receives from his social environment and his own self-assessment of abilities on the basis of objective information provided by his academic performance" (1975:348).

Porter et al. illustrate this path:

> the way a person performs in school contributes to the perceptions that his parents have of his capabilities. This in turn causes his parents to have particular aspirations for him, and these aspirations as perceived by the individual contribute to self-image, which affects his own aspirations....At the same time, his school performance contributes to the image he has of his academic ability and thence to his educational aspirations [his self-assessment of abilites based on academic performance] (1982:122-123).

Reitzes and Mutran (1980) in a study of self-conceptions as factors influencing educational expectation based on questionnaire responses from 396 students in a midwestern university in the United States, have concluded that those students with high self-esteem and self-confidence in their abilities had the highest expectations. Similar findings were reported by Anisef (1973) in a sample of high school students in Ontario.

In demonstrating the relationship between educational aspirations and self-concept of ability, Porter et al. offer some interesting results: "65 per cent of grade 10 students with high self-concept of ability wanted to go to university, and only six per cent of those with low self-concept had such aspirations" (1982:88). Consequently, "only five per cent with high self-concept of ability wanted to go to work, compared to 34 per cent with low self-concept" (1982:88).

Furthermore, the authors reported that 19 per cent of females and 25 per cent of males in the five-year high school programme (a programme that often leads to some form of post-secondary education) believed that they were very able. In grade 12, for example, the figures were even more accentuated. Males who believed that they were very able accounted for 31 per cent, while females accounted for only 15 per cent. The authors measured self-concept through a series of questions utilizing a five-point ordinal scale. Some examples of the questions were: "How do you rate yourself in school ability compared with those in your class at school? Forget for a moment how others grade your work. In your own opinion how good do you think your work is?" (Porter et al., 1982:47-78).

The results of differentiating socialization patterns for males as opposed to females were also evident in other studies. Jacobs, in a study of aspirations and occupations of a selected group of women in the United States, writes: "Early life socialization is often accorded an important if not decisive role in shaping the labour force experiences of women" (1987:122). What may be implied here is that early socialization is important to one's perception of what one is capable of doing. As such, if given the right opportunity, students, regardless of inadequacies in their backgrounds, should fare very well if they have a strong belief in their capabilities.

Maxwell and Maxwell, in a study of educational and occupational aspirations among private school females in Ontario, propose that "although women may pursue post-secondary education and post-university education, they are less likely than males to choose the type of education that will lead them to high-status occupations or high earning" (1984:378).

Wilson and Portes, commenting on the importance of self-esteem and self-concept of ability in relation to educational aspirations, elaborate: "A person develops and adjusts his aspirations in accordance with both the evaluation he receives from his social environment and his own self-assessment of abilities on the basis of objective information provided by his academic performance" (1975:357).

This "interactionist" premise in the explanation of self-concept is succinctly stated by Reitzes and Mutran: "individuals may use self-concepts to interpret their behaviour and these concepts may serve as motivational forces" (1980:31).

As far as immigrant youth are concerned, Akoodie (1984) proposes that positive and/or negative self-concept is related to the actual social experience the youth encounters. For the immigrant youth this is particularly important since being "accepted" by the youth of the host society means an easier integration. Akoodie continues:

> In seeking acceptance from the majority group and their peers, immigrant children frequently find rejection and may become despondent and suffer ambivalence, inferiority, hypersensitivity, and guilt feelings arising from giving up their identification with the family. The adjustment is often disruptive, leading to personal disorganization, loss of identiy and lack of self-confidence....individuals need a sense of identity with their heritage and culture of their group because it is through positive emotional and cultural experience that a healthy self-concept develops (1984:254).

PERCEPTION OF OPPORTUNITY

Whatever the motivational forces, which exist for the individual, the literature has also shown that they may be curtailed by the actor's perception of opportunity. This variable is an important predictor of the educational aspiration-formation process. This is especially evident in the literature dealing with comparisons of aspirations between disadvantaged ethnic groups, low socio-economic background aggregates, and high-status, high socio-economic background collectivities.

In a study of 1202 elementary school students in the southern United States, Howell and Frese (1979) postulate that educational aspirations among black males and females are higher than those of the white students within the sample. However, Kerckhoff and Campbell view the above findings as somewhat unrealistic, especially when taking into consideration the group's perception of opportunity: "for a middle-class child to go to college, he need only combine desire with a modicum of academic performance" (1975:703). However, if the child was black or from a lower socio-economic background, other variables such as source of funds may be major precursors to post-secondary aspirations. Stafford et al. (1984) propose that

> an individual will purchase a college education if the present value of the expected social and economic benefits resulting

from the education exceeds the present cost of education. The expected benefits include the additional lifetime income and social and intellectual rewards a person might expect to receive (1984:593).

If the individual's perception of opportunity structure is perceived to be fatalistic the result may be that the disadvantaged groups may curtail their aspirations and settle for lower attainments then their seemingly advantaged counterparts.

This perception of a closed opportunity structure may be ingrained in the early socialization practices that have differed along ethnic and socio-economic lines and, as some have suggested (Deosoran, 1975; Calliste, 1980; Jansen, 1981), have been upheld through educational institution stereotyping. This area will be explored in the next section.

SUMMARY

It has become evident that the educational aspiration-formation process for adolescents is characterized by a number of influences. Various authors have proposed and tested the effects of such variables as the influences of one's girlfriend or regional origin, to variables such as one's self-concept of ability and perception of opportunity.

Concurrently, factors such as gender, socio-economic background, and ethnic affiliation have been found to significantly affect educational aspirations, and their consequent translation into educational achievement.

Adolescence, which may be characterized as a period in life that is filled with social and personal strife, may be more chaotic if one's educational potential is hindered, particularly if the individual has high aspirations but cannot actualize them. Furthermore, if his or her aspirations cannot be translated into educational success as a result of ascriptive obstacles, then the educational system, which may be considered as a second most important socializing agent, would certainly be under question.

The literature that has been presented, though seemingly inexhaustive, nevertheless presents a strong argument for the influences of ascriptive variables. Thus, so far, we may infer that in Canada in general, and Ontario in particular, young people who come from select social and ethnic backgrounds and who are males tend to have a much better chance at enhancing their educational aspirations than their disadvantaged counterparts.

CHAPTER TWO

Equality of Opportunity? Perceptions of the Educational System

Education remains a very important precursor to occupational attainment in Canada. As a result it has occupied a central role in the analysis of social mobility and stratification. Some have argued (Jencks, 1972), that ideally, educational aspirations and attainment should only be affected by the student's interest, ability, and potential. If the student wishes to become a teacher, electrician, or assembly line worker, he or she should strive towards these goals without encountering pressures associated with being a part of a select social class, gender, or ethnic group. The role of the secondary and post-secondary institutions should be to search out and develop the needed talent that could be certified to perform at various levels in the occupational hierarchy.

Krauze and Slomczynski, commenting on this notion of "meritocracy" note:

> the concept of meritocracy refers to a large-scale social system in which a positive relationship exists between "merit" and such commonly desired values as income, power, and prestige. Merit is usually indicated by IQ and other tests of cognitive skills, or by educational attainment. ...Individuals obtain income, power, and prestige not directly, but through

occupational positions to which these rewards are attached. Therefore, the extent to which meritocracy is achieved can be expressed in terms of matching individuals with a given level of merit to occupational positions with given levels of rewards (1985:624).

As far as the educational system and its relationship to IQ meritocracy, "formal education is assigned the task of sorting, selecting, and channelling individuals according to their cognitive competence" (Krauz and Slomczynski, 1985:624).

A study based on a sample of Americans in the labour force in 1977 offers a number of interesting observations. Generally, as far as the United States is concerned, meritocracy is not a reality. Computing correlations between status and education for employed males in 1920, 1940, 1960, and 1977, Krauze and Slomczynski suggest that "meritocracy, viewed as an ideological legitimization of the technocratic system, did not turn into a self-fulfilling prophecy" (1985:634).

The authors refute Ornstein's (1986) notion that meritocratic stratification has replaced ascriptive stratification, particularly with the view that educational credentials are in the forefront of social status stratification. They propose that while the educational system has indeed expanded, as a result of broadening occupational opportunities that in turn offered each individual a better chance at mobility, nevertheless, "controlling for changes in the distribution constraints on education and status, we find no support for the trend to meritocracy in American society" (Krauz and Slomczynski, 1985:639).

Moreover, "insofar as the level of education has a measurable relationship to social class, any policies or programs promoting meritocracy fulfill class interests to differing extents for different classes since their ensuing benefits or losses differ" (Krauze and Slomczynski, 1985:640).

Notwithstanding, the educational system often perpetuates ascent along ascriptively related factors such as socio-economic background and ethnicity. Husen contends: "Educational systems have to a varying extent built-in mechanisms which exert restraints in terms of promoting the development of talent and are biased against students of disadvantaged backgrounds" (1974:135).

It seems that schools tend to produce a stratified social structure that benefits the advantaged members of the population. Nelson's analogy illustrates this point:

> Into the hooper is fed the raw material children. As they progress through dials and gauges of the enclosed box [the school] they are pulled, pushed, and squeezed into channels leading to specific outlet tubes. The resulting produce is spewed into different baskets marked blue collar, white collar, managerial, professional...rejects (1974:147).

In the case of Ontario's educational system, middle-class children are judged more educable by middle-class teachers who utilize a middle-class language and apply middle-class standards. Accordingly, students from the lower classes, select ethnic backgrounds, or newly arrived immigrants, being at a cognitive and linguistic disadvantage, are likely to suffer from lowered self-esteem and complexes of inferiority. Rudd illustrates: "Working class [immigrant] children have less facility in their use of language than those of the middle class, and especially the professional class, and so are at a disadvantage wherever the use of words [school] is important, especially in the discussion of ideas" (1984:32). The resulting anxiety caused by the perceived lack of control over their environment may cause the students to opt for the workforce at the earliest opportune moment.

Such a disadvantaged student faces further obstacles within the middle-class milieu, which unconsciously promotes the student's feeling of inadequacy by constant comparison with the advantaged upper-class schoolmate, who, as Murphy contends, brings into the classroom a wealth of cultural and linguistic capital that is more harmonious with the school's demands (1977:208).

Porter et al. suggests that

> to the extent that the school system, particularly in its academically oriented programs, dispenses the high culture of the society, it is for the middle-class family an adjunct to their own socialization.... Where the school dispenses high culture to those who, because of their social class position, are already acquainted with it, there is general compatibility between home and school (1982:87).

The results of their analysis of Ontario high school students show that 58 per cent of upper-class students who were exposed to high cultural enrichment aspired to attend university. The comparable figure for the lower-class was 34 per cent (1982:89-90).

Consequently, as DiMaggio and Mohr argue:

> the ability to participate in a prestigious [upper class] status culture, then, enables individuals to survive ... the routine assessment of social competence and to sustain relationships with those in control [the education system] of allocation of rewards that constitute the stratification process" (1985:1236).

Immigrant students who happen to belong to the lower class find themselves in a disheartening situation, not receiving the needed encouragement at home or at school. Conditioned by the perceived lack of opportunity within an unjust society, they may be forced to settle for jobs which are below their ability.

Prestigious jobs are perceived as unobtainable, and students conditioned by their background may wholeheartedly accept their ascribed niche in the social structure. James (1986) suggests that minority students nurture high educational and occupational aspirations in anticipation of their respective position in the social structure. He writes: "they [the minorities] hold high aspirations knowing that they will not achieve their goal. Yet they are prepared to hold such aspirations reasoning that they have to aim high in order to compensate for the discrimination they will face later" (1986:74). It appears then, that aspirations and attainment are more likely based on an individual's origin than on his or her talent or ability.

Commenting on the structure of inequality or equality of opportunity, we should, at this time, elaborate on what the literature views as inequality or equality of opportunity and its relationship to inequality or equality of condition. Porter et al. propose that a "commitment to equality necessitates a society in which each person has the opportunity to develop his talents and to strive for unequal rewards" (1982:5). Therefore, equality of opportunity does not necessarily lead to an "equal society." Consequently, equality of condition reflects the notion that "individuals are different and their treatment should be determined by their particular interests" (1982:4). They conclude that equality of condition leads to equality of opportunity.

As far as equal educational opportunity is concerned, Oakes proposes that

> equal educational opportunity means equal opportunity to develop quite fixed individual potential [intelligence and

abilities] to its limit through individual effort in school, regardless of such irrelevant background characteristics as race, [ethnicity], class, and gender" (1986:61).

Oakes adds that both society and the individual would benefit if the individual was allowed to optimize his or her potential. She comments that the equality of opportunity would provide the individual with

> fair access to the world of work by providing fair access to the technical knowledge, the skills, and the attitudes that make possible the production of goods and services. Work is the way to attain the material and non-material resources of society [wealth, prestige, power]. For society equal educational opportunity means that individuals' talents are developed for the benefit of all (1986:61).

However, Oakes states that no reforms have managed to bring the educational system within boundaries of anything that resembles equality of opportunity. She proposes that the schooling process is camouflaged in meritocracy and characterized by Anglo conformity:

> Deemed "excellent" in the reform rhetoric, this mode of schooling has historically restricted both access to education and achievement of ethnic minority and poor children. Well intentioned, progressive reformers have, at times, succeeded in mitigating the injustice inherent in these forms, even so, the current politics of social conservatism, far from inventing new inequities, appear to be largely capitalizing on endemic ones (1986:61).

Thus, the system upheld and continues to uphold traditional class-based principles. For upward social mobility, it is of inordinate importance. Although it continues to favour students from particular backgrounds, one should note that not all jobs are qualification-dependent. In many instances, nepotism is an overriding factor in job acquisitions.

The university-educated parent of an upper-class student will, as Jansen suggests:

> very likely try harder to persuade his child to continue his education. He cannot conceive of his child as a garbageman.

> The garbageman might prefer his son to do better than he himself has, but he will not be too disconsolate if he does not. He knows that while it is perhaps not ideal, such a life is viable. Besides, he has his own self-respect. If he deprecates too strongly his own position he is admitting failure. The son, too, while ideally preferring to be a college professor, is not likely to feel it is the end of the world if he ends up doing as his father did" (Jansen, 1981:17).

Accordingly, one can attest to the notion that the standards of performance at some social levels, in formal (school) or informal (home) settings reflect the power of the dominant group whose norms and values are taught and upheld by the educational system. This power structure is carried over into the occupational field where "members of the Canadian economic elite are recruited in disproportionate numbers from among sons of upper-class persons," thereby indicating the importance of ascribed status (Calliste, 1980:34).

For working-class children the perception of occupational reality is different. Gaskell and Lazerson (1980-81), gathering data from a longitudinal study of high school students in Vancouver, British Columbia in 1977, suggest that working-class youth are quite content with blue-collar work, in essence, following in their parents' footsteps. Not only are they appeased, but they seem to be overly

> optimistic about the satisfaction work can provide, even while they criticize and complain about their jobs. They are also critical of their schooling, but they accept as fair the advantage that schooling provides in the labour market.... Their frustration and criticisms do not lead them to reject, in any fundamental way, the way education and work are organized. The future is bright, even with the society the way it is (1980-81:93).

Subsequently, one can illustrate the inequality of opportunity structure and its effects on educational aspirations through an examination of socialization practices and value transmission within certain social milieux and select ethnic groups. Socialization, may universally be defined as a process of learning. Specifically, it is "the process whereby the individual learns techniques and acquires traits which enable him to achieve adult statuses and play concomitant roles" (Tomovic, 1979:160).

Porter et al. illustrate this process by suggesting that

> socialization begins in infancy and continues through childhood to embrace a multitude of experiences in the home, in school, and in age-peer groups. ...The child, by interacting with others, learns "appropriate" social roles and the rules of behaviour that support them, that is, the behavioural norms of the groups in which he finds himself (1982:25).

The authors continue:

> these norms and values in turn reflect those of the wide social milieux neighbourhoods, social classes, and religious sub-cultures. ... Through interacting with others the child learns to conform to the behaviour that others expect of him.... The adults are the socializers and the child the socializee. ... [eventually the] individual learns that conformity to rules brings rewards while non-conformity results in punishments and deprivations (1982:25-26).

Consequently, the individual has to learn "about those statuses towards which he may realistically aspire" (Tomovic, 1979:160). Hence, it seems that not only the educational system, but the society in general, has built-in mechanisms that differentiate individuals along ascriptive norms over which they have no power. It seems that, as Jansen points out, it is the ascriptive status factors that discourage children from striving for success and a better situation in Canadian society (1981:12).

Still, occupational and educational stratification, in any society, may be viewed as a natural phenomenon designed to differentiate between actors' performance along the hierarchical range of educational and occupational positions. In other words, not every actor aspires towards the same educational goal. Based on the notions of "meritocratic" theory, specific talents lead to specific aspirations and attainments.

This type of occurrence, based on the association between talent, ambition, and aspirations, would be an example of a free society or one where one could encounter equality of opportunity. If post-secondary education was free for all, then the resulting educational stratification would be based along meritocratic notions. The introduction of post-secondary schools' tuition fees, in concert with arbitrarily imposed entrance criteria, could form an obstacle to a number of otherwise eligible candidates.

At the same time, the disadvantaged members within certain groups are socialized through a number of institutions, the most important being the family. This socialization leads to their acceptance of limitations as normal and thereby to their opting for a lower level of expectation. A child with high educational aspirations, living in a poor rural family, and seeing the accomplishments of his or her father who labours as a farmer's helper, may succumb to the same way of life after reviewing the obstacles that may stand in the way of his or her post-secondary schooling.

A theoretically impressive trend in education began to develop in the 1950s. A quote from a paper delivered at a Canadian education conference in 1958 illustrated that educational opportunity should be

> extended to every young person as an inalienable human right. To make sure that this opportunity is available, public schools are supported everywhere at public expense.... Beyond the years of compulsory attendance, free education is also available in public secondary schools, vocational schools, adult classes, colleges, and universities (Porter et al., 1982:21-22).

During the 1960s it was further argued that education should be a universal right. To alleviate post-secondary entrance status problems for those with economic difficulties, provinces introduced programmes such as the "Ontario Student Award Programme."

The Ontario Student Award Programme may, nevertheless, be utilized in most instances by those students who, to a greater extent, are middle class with minor financial difficulties. It would be unrealistic to expect the student to survive solely on the amount that he or she may receive in any given year. Furthermore, the assistance programme lasts for a maximum period of four years, thereby possibly precluding the student's aspirations for professional schools (graduate, law, teaching, medicine). Finally, if the student manages to survive on the very limited income, he or she has to repay the loans upon graduation.

Consequently, it is an unrealistic demand of the universities (in concert with the provincial government) to expect that a full-time graduate student, receiving funding from the university, is not expected to be employed outside the institution. This would be extremely difficult for someone who is receiving a grant and/or a salary (obtained for services as a teaching assistant) in the vicinity of seven thousand (1989) dollars. One may not be able to imagine the difficulties imposed on a married couple, with a child, who are enrolled in and/or aspiring to graduate education. Therefore, in view of the present graduate employment trends, much difficulty may be encountered in attempting to repay the incurred loans.

The government's attempt at equalizing post-secondary entrance status for all students is limited. Rather, it is an inducement to those who may be considered marginally advantaged. In essence, it is a show, illustrating an attempt at an egalitarian opportunity structure. Accordingly, its accomplishments create deepened cleavages between those who have high-aspirations/high-expectations and those who have high-aspirations/low-expectations.

Preferring to comment on the American experience, (although reflective of Canadian as well), Oakes writes: "reforms will work largely to the advantage of those who are already well-off. Through differentiated schooling experiences, attention will be turned from the difficulties of those served less well by schools" (1986:77).

As was previously mentioned, the most important socializing agent within all industrialized nations is the family. Being a member of a particular ethnic group or social class, the family imposes social norms and values upon its children so they can acquire their respective roles within the social hierarchy.

The inequality is maintained within this social hierarchy through what Calliste (1980) labels "particularistic-ascriptive transmission." In view of education, this transmission occurs through the importance the family places upon it. Families from select ethnic backgrounds, for example those who value high educational achievement who are members of the middle or upper class, are likely to transmit positive educational values to their children. On the other hand, families within the lower class or those of particular ethnic backgrounds who do not value high educational achievement may tend to transmit negative educational values to their children.

The child belonging to a middle-class family is often urged to do well in school. He or she is stimulated through the use of educational games and is led to believe that school offers social mobility. He or she is prepared for high aspirations and attainments through the inculcation of his or her parents' middle-class values. However, as the reviewed literature has illustrated, intergenerational immobility occurs particularly for those students who do not have roots in the middle class or who are from select ethnic groups. This highlights the point that in the secondary school system, children tend to be streamed into occupational tracks similar to those that their significant elders held.

What is stressed here is that once again the educational system reinforces certain social stereotypes, allowing very little intergenerational mobility. Although feasible for advantaged children, since they will at least achieve a certain degree of prestige allotted to middle-class occupations, it becomes another obstacle to the disadvantaged child.

Danziger, in a study of socialization of immigrant children, points out the effects of negative value transmission on a sample of Italian high school students. He suggested that these children were not encouraged to strive towards achievement or success through schooling. Rather, they were persuaded to enter the workforce at the first opportunity in order to contribute to the family income (1975:129-131). It should be noted that in Danziger's sample only ten per cent of the parents had formal education beyond compulsory education. Furthermore, the background of the parents was overwhelmingly rural.

Nevertheless, this part of the sample was considered by Danziger to reflect the ideology of what he termed "low acculturation groups," suggesting the lack of social networks outside the Italian community.

On the other hand, the "highly acculturated" immigrants from Italy tended to inculcate high educational ideals into their children. Moreover, these aspirations were strongly nourished towards post-secondary educational goals. Maykovich (1975), in a comparison study of Italian and Japanese Canadians, echoes the importance of rural-urban differences.

Jansen's (1981) study on educational mobility of Italians shows that while descendents of Italian parentage show significant educational gains over their parents, they are, nevertheless, underrepresented in post-secondary institutions. He states that the basic reason for the educational gain is the length of compulsory schooling in Canada, which is far greater than in Italy. Thus, "looking beyond compulsory-age or to post-secondary education, Italians fall short of the national proportions at school than comparable ethnic and mother-tongue groups" (Jansen, 1981:50).

Richmond's (1986) paper "Ethnogenerational Variation in Educational Achievment," was based on a Toronto survey undertaken in 1982. He proposed that those students comprising the second generation fared (educationally) much better than their immigrant predecessors. Particularly, as far as Italians are concerned, he shows that only 5 per cent of first generation Italian immigrants had some university education in 1971, compared with 9 per cent of the second and 11 per cent of the third plus. By 1981, there was little change among foreign-born Italians as a whole, only 6.3 per cent men and 3.7 per cent women reporting some university training [with or without a degree], but the proportion was 29 per cent of men and 16.3 per cent of women among those who had arrived as children and who were, by then, 25 to 34 years of age (1986:3-4).

Still, it seems evident that ethnicity has a direct effect on educational aspirations and attainment. The question that remains unanswered is to what extent the aspirations are inherent in and dictated by the ethnic group. In other words, it seems that the majority of studies on Italians and other disadvantaged ethnic groups claim that these groups promote post-secondary educational aspirations within their offspring. Yet the results show an underrepresented number of these students in post-secondary institutions. Thus, the issue that needs to be addressed with Italian and other similar groups is the one that would deal with achievement orientation and its relationship to aspiration formation.

Hence, in interpreting these findings one could easily conclude that the general consensus among the group is their perceived inability to succeed at a post-secondary education (university) level. Or perhaps, there exist external influences over which the group has no control, ones that are acting to negate high aspirations.

Within the "particularistic-ascriptive" sphere of Canadian society, one would have to conclude that the latter is the case. If a student is a member of a particular social status group whose norms and values reflect those of the dominant group, then it is likely that he or she will be motivated towards high educational aspirations and attainment. A student belonging to a minority group is faced with a greater obstacle — lack of opportunity.

As Calliste (1980) suggests, it becomes appropriate for the family to transmit certain values to its younger members, which may prove to be advantageous to educational aspirations or attainment, depending on the congruity towards the values of the Canadian elite. She further contends that

> in industrial society rewards are distributed through attainment, but attainment in turn is largely dictated by

ascriptive particularistic criteria. Those of higher socio-economic status transmit to their heirs, with the support of the educational system, the social graces and the cognitive skills necessary for success in the occupational world (1980:48-49).

Therefore, one can see that, as Oakes contends, the American — and in the view of this writer, Canadian — society perpetuates the "neo-conservative reassertion of the turn-of-the-century values and belief...beliefs that emerge virtually unaltered in the proposals for reform" (1986:72).

Oakes further suggests that an obstacle to educational and, consequently, occupational success rests on laurels of Anglo conformity. "Definitions of quality and standards [in schooling] are those that have historically served to discriminate against youngsters who are poor or members of ethnic minorities" (1986:73). She elaborates: "There is no [real] recognition of the unique contributions of different cultures or of the special problems that arise from a history of discrimination" (1986:73).

Certainly, in Canada, this thesis of Anglo conformity is cognizant of the proposals of Porter's now famous "Vertical Mosaic." Among other things, he suggests that in order to optimize one's educational and, more precisely, occupational potential, the immigrant group should most closely resemble the dominant Anglo group. Clifton elaborates:

> Children socialized within ethnic subcultures have developed abilities, aspirations, and motivations which match certain occupational status positions within society. In turn, the shaping of abilities, aspirations, and motivation within ethnic subcultures could set limits on educational achievement which could also set limits on occupational achievement (1984:1).

Evidently, the literature seems to concur with the fact that particular ethnic backgrounds can have an influence on the optimization of one's educational and occupational potential.

An editorial reflecting the Toronto experience, appearing in the *Toronto Star*, illustrates: "it's necessary to reflect on ... ongoing struggles of non-Anglo minorities for acceptance and for equal opportunity to participate fully in economic, political, social, and other aspects of Metro life. ... [Still there are] hidden prejudices, subtle discriminations, and value clashes. Some groups are poorly represented in managerial and executive positions and in the professions" (1985, Dec. 26:A26).

Porter suggests that "reference groups can be mobility-inhibiting, particularly in a society where class is reinforced by ethnicity [Canada]" (1979:77). This is of particular importance to a member of a disadvantaged ethnic group, since its members could very easily align their aspirations with the norms of the group and, in most instances, opt for early school leaving. These individuals usually feel that the school will not influence them into staying. Moreover,

> the more a minority group turns upon itself and concentrates on making its position strong, the more it costs its members in terms of their chances to make their way as individuals in the larger system.... Among ethnic minority groups which strive to maintain language and other distinctions, motivation to aspire to high-ranking social and economic positions in the larger system will be weak, unless it is characteristic of the ethnic groups to put a special stress on educational and vocational achievement (Porter, 1979:126).

At this point we will turn our attention to the influence of the educational system on educational aspirations and particularly the aspiration formation of "disadvantaged" youth. Primarily we will comment on the extent that the school officials, teachers, counsellors, and principals uphold the traditional "Anglo conformist" views of education.

Oakes (1986) comments on the differences with which school tracks (in Canada the parallel could be defined as various streams, for example, level II through level V, with level V being university bound) treat minority groups. Illustrating the findings of an American sample she proposed that

> there [are] considerable differences in the kinds of knowledge students in various tracks had access to.... Students in high-track classes were exposed to "high status" content.... The schools made decisions about the appropriateness of various topics and skills and, in doing so, limited sharply what some students would learn. The lower the track, the greater the limits.... In the high-track classes, teachers were perceived as more concerned and supportive; ... Students in low-track classes more often characterized their teachers as punitive (1986:63).

Reflecting the Canadian experience, Porter et al. propose that

> school personnel may be more important to lower-class [and disadvantaged ethnic groups] than upper-middle-class students since the former, coming from economically and culturally deprived families, are the most obvious target for information and counselling concerning educational and economic opportunities (1982:138).

Consequently, one would expect that as far as Canada, and particularly Ontario, is concerned, school tracks (for Ontario viewed as level III, IV, or level V) should be decided based on "merit." This placing is considered to be very important, since, if one chooses or is placed in the wrong stream (track), their opportunity for attending university would be greatly curtailed. Porter et al. (1982) point out that of their sample 60 per cent of lower-class students were placed in the possible university stream. Comparably, 80 per cent of upper-middle-class students were placed in the university stream (Porter et al., 1982:204).

They contend that misplacement may well be the result of "the type of slippage which is bound to occur in the large bureaucratic system" (Porter et al., 1982:199). Oakes suggests:

> it is likely that the differential socialization of children from various racial, [ethnic], and economic backgrounds results from the programmatic differences they experience. ... If the access to certain kinds of knowledge or organizational arrangements is restricted for some students and enhanced for others, schools cannot be said to be providing equal educational opportunity (1983:348).

Moreover, "the well-off ... do not need special rules to favour them; the universalistic rules of the present system favour them quite well enough" (Porter et al., 1982:208). A rather interesting anecdote appeared in Canada's national newspaper, *The Globe and Mail*, which illustrates the issue quite effectively:

> Why, the head of a French business school was once asked, do you accept so many offspring of the wealthy and powerful

when they do not measure academically? His typical Gallic response: These people will be in charge one day anyway; we might as well try to teach them something along the way (1986, Sep. 10:A1).

Nevertheless:

in the name of equal opportunity, track levels in schools, reflective of social and economic groupings in society, are provided with differential access to school opportunities that is likely to maintain, or increase, rather than erase, the inequities in the larger social structure (Oakes, 1986:63).

The extent to which the schools are trying to alleviate this problem is implied in Oakes' article. She suggests that not only is there a decrease in the university enrollment of minorities, but, as well, this aggregate is underrepresented in professional and post-graduate education (1986:77). The reviewed literature suggests that school personnel are instrumental in the formation and eventual optimization of one's educational aspirations. At the same time, it is argued, school personnel are consciously and/or unconsciously biased against youth from disadvantaged ethnic and economic groups.

Lareau proposes that "social profitability of middle-class arrangements is tied to the schools' definition of the proper family-school relationship" (1987:82). As such, it may be possible, as some literature (Lightfoot, 1985) has shown, that secondary schools favour children of middle-class families and disfavour those from disadvantaged backgrounds. Lareau, in studying the relationship between school personnel and parents in a working-class neighbourhood consisting of predominantly Hispanic, Asian, Black, and Vietnamese families in the northern United States, writes:

Teachers and administrators spoke of being "partners" with parents, and they stressed the need to maintain good communication, but it was clear that they desired parents to defer to their professional expertise.... Nor did principals welcome parents' opinions that a teacher was a bad teacher and should be fired (1986:76).

Higginbotham (1985), in a study of college attendance barriers to Blacks in the United States, comments: "Black parents, concerned with the educational attainment of their children cannot relax and trust the public school system to fairly assess their children's talents and to prepare them to assume adult roles in line with their abilities" (1985:94).

In view of such events, and particularly as a result of historical tradition, working-class and disadvantaged ethnic groups view the teacher with very high regard. "Just as they depended on doctors to heal their children, they depended on teachers to educate them" (Lareau, 1987:81).

Although most teachers are doing their jobs, some are not focusing enough attention on developing sensitivities towards those students who do not fit into the "middle-class ideology." Rather than accepting the fact that someone may be different, they are more interested in creating some sort of a "normalized" educational environment, which produces the all encompassing "average type" against whom society compares itself. To paraphrase a teacher's report card comment, "your son walks to a beat of a different drummer, but that's okay, because by the end of the school year, we will have him walking to the right beat."

Evidence suggests that the ethnic background of a child may be instrumental in the way he or she will be treated in the classroom. Clifton et al. propose that gender and ethnicity are "two of the most common sources of information from which a teacher can form impressions of students. The sex of a student is easily determined and ethnicity is often identified by racial and cultural characteristics, names, and languages" (1986:58). Furthermore, it is argued that "schools play a major role in perpetuating the existing social stratification system, partly because teachers assume that children with certain ascribed characteristics learn faster than children with other ascribed characteristics" (Guppy et al., 1984:60).

What the preceding quote implies is that, for the child with the right attributes, the school teacher will work on enhancing their optimum potential. For a student from a disadvantaged background, the opposite may be the case. Thus, the student with high aspirations who comes from a disadvantaged ethnic background may be led to believe that his or her aspirations are unrealistic and that the best thing to do would be to adjust one's aspirations to one's ascriptive background.

For most students the anxieties of teenage years may affect one's educational life decision, since they may be influenced by obstacles over which they have no power. A teacher's statement that a student is not capable may cause the student to accept the decision as final, which in turn may result in a self-fulfilling prophecy. The student is often led to believe that if the teacher says that he or she cannot handle the advanced programme, then perhaps a lower stream would be more beneficial. Clifton et al. point out that

> differences in teachers' expectations may facilitate differential learning, since differential expectations probably affect the feedback and evaluation that teachers give to their students. ...Teachers may have more positive interactions with students for whom they have high expectations. As a result, high expectations enhance learning, and low expectations inhibit learning (1986:66).

Thus the teacher, who, in essence, should work towards eradicating the inequalities due to personal background, in some cases actually contributes to make the ascriptive cleavages even deeper. One need only look at the results of the now famous study of this nature, "The Pygmalion in the Classroom."

Indeed, Clifton et al. (1986), in a study of teachers' expectations of an ethnically diverse aggregate consisting of British, Native Canadian, Filipino, French, German, and Portuguese junior high school students in Winnipeg, Manitoba, report that teachers expectations in relation to the students' cognitive ability are, among other things, influenced by the students' ethnic background. They report that of the total sample, teachers had lower expectations of students from Native Canadian, Portuguese, and French backgrounds (1986:64). Our educators, coming from all sorts of social, economic, and cultural backgrounds are, in general, ill-equipped to deal with students from different social, cultural, and economic backgrounds. Rather than trying to integrate the benefits of "multicultural" diversities, they are quick to point out that such reforms as the introduction of heritage language classes (introduced in the parliament of Ontario) in the daily school curriculum, are detrimental to their "standardized programmes."

Hence, reforms that could contribute to the self-confidence of a child coming from a "non-Anglo" background are met with opposition, thus once again contributing to the notion that in order to optimize one's educational potential one has to reflect and/or assimilate into the values of the dominant "Anglo" group.

Nevertheless, Canadian studies (Anisef et al., 1985; Richmond, 1986) have, however, reported that a great deal of democratization has taken place in the post-secondary education system, and that there is a significant increase in intergenerational educational mobility. However, this "educational democratization" for those coming from select backgrounds may well be in the form of increased enrollment in post-secondary non-university streams.

Guppy commented on the educational expansion that occurred this century in Canada and its relationship to educational opportunity: "the chances for obtaining a university degree have been consistently better for middle- and upper-class English-Canadian males. The democratization of post-secondary education ... resulted mainly from expansion of opportunities presented by the opening of numerous colleges and institutes" (1984:89). As far as democratization is concerned: "educational chances are currently unequal. The policy relevance of such inequality in the distribution of opportunity for higher education is difficult to overestimate. Increasingly occupational training, certification, and selection occurs through the educational system, particularly in post-secondary institutions" (1984:89).

Furthermore:

> to the extent that this function is enhanced through time, while socially based disparities in opportunities for higher education [especially university] continue, then individual life chances must, remain unequal. If higher education is contingent upon social attributes unrelated to academic ability — such as gender, ethnicity, and class — then in the end we waste precious resources by excluding gifted individuals (Guppy, 1984:89).

Consequently, the policy of multiculturalism that was introduced in Canada guarantees each ethnic group the right to maintain its traditions and heritage without the fear that their cultural background will hinder their rights to optimize their educational and occupational goals. Concurrently, the Canadian constitution has upheld those rights and has entrenched in its laws that every person will have an opportunity to, on the basis of talent and ability, optimize their life goals.

If someone's ethnic affiliation precludes their right to knowledge, then the

> Canadian policy of multiculturalism, which states that ethnicity must not be a criterion in determining the benefits, including feedback and evaluations from teachers, individuals receive

within schools or other social institutions.... differential expectations based on ascribed criteria, such as ethnicity [socio-economic background] and sex, violate the norm of universalism, which states that all students should be treated as equal members of age-grade cohorts except as they differ in ability and performance (Clifton et al., 1986:66).

SUMMARY

It was the intent of this chapter to determine the extent to which the educational system is responsible for upholding social stratification on the basis of ascriptive variables, such as one's socio-economic background, gender, and ethnic affiliation. The literature reviewed demonstrates that the educational system upholds the notion that persons from select ethnic backgrounds can only optimize their educational and occupational potentials if they assimilate into the norms and the values of the dominant Anglo group.

While in Canada, legislation instituted in the Canadian constitution guarantees each individual a right to practice and live according to his or her cultural heritage, that right may be detrimental to the optimization of one's educational potential.

Furthermore, the educational institution, considered to be the second most important socializing agent, is not doing enough to eradicate the institutional bias towards those students who may be lacking cognitive and social skills and are depending on the educational system to guide them through these inadequacies. Rather, the system further instills in them the "educational inability complex" that may consequently inhibit their post-secondary aspirations and eventual attainment.

As we have shown, all attempts at reform have benefited select ascriptive groups. "Meritocracy" has not replaced ascription. Educationally, one may have high aspirations, however, these aspirations have a much better chance of being turned into optimal attainment if the actor is not from a disadvantaged background, regardless of academic talent, ability, or interest.

CHAPTER THREE

Croatians

Studies in the field of education have often categorized smaller ethnic groups by geographic regions. Only a few are selected for individualized research. These groups are usually the ones that are visibly either on the top or the bottom of the educational hierarchy. Other ethnic or racial groups are at times clustered into geographically generic enclaves such as South Europeans, West Indians, and Eastern Europeans. Whatever the reasons for the clustering, it is important that researchers study as many ethnic groups as possible in order to facilitate a just and fair educational policy.

Because of the lack of research on this group, the purpose of this chapter is to familiarize the reader with Croatian history and migration patterns, particularly as they relate to Canada. We should start with an extremely brief and crudely general historiographical account of Croatia.

CROATIA

Croatian history can roughly be divided into five periods, with the first lasting from 680 A.D. to 1100 A.D. In the early part of this period it is believed that Croatians accepted Christianity (Herman, 1978:19). It should also be noted that Croatians were among the first people at the time to be allowed to, in the celebrations of their newly embraced religion, say mass in their native Croatian, known as "glagolica."

During this time, and more precisely around 923 A.D., Croatia became an independent kingdom and crowned Duke Tomislav as the first king of Croatia. The period was marred by internal strife and the throne was exchanged a number of times.

Its boundaries, as many world geographical boundaries, were redrawn on numerous occasions. Generally, as is the agreement among consulted literature (Herman, 1978), Croatians are located in the Balkan peninsula. The Croatian northern border with Hungary was the river Drava. The river Drina formed the natural boundary with its eastern neighbour Serbia. To the northwest, the Slovenian Alps became its border with Slovenia. Its southwestern border is the Adriatic Sea.

The second Croatian epoch lasted from 1102 to 1526 and was marked by the rule of Hungarian aristocracy over Croatia (Herman, 1978). During this time there were numerous struggles with the Turks, who at the time conquered Croatian's Bosnian neighbours. The Turkish influence was overwhelming, forcing many Croats to convert to Islam as a way of saving their lives. Croats, under the rule of another occupier (Hungary), nevertheless fought the Turks, limiting their domination of Croatian lands.

The third period lasted from 1526 to 1790 and was marked by the Croatian resistance to "Germanization" by the strong Austrian aristocracy. Hoping for independence from the Austrians, Croatian nobility sought alliance with the Hungarians, who expressed interest in offering Croats full autonomy (Herman, 1978:22).

The fourth period from 1790 to 1918, was characterized by not only increased Austrian domination, but Hungarian domination as well. Both countries wanted to rule Croatia. In 1867, Austria, as Herman (1978) points out, divided its power over Croatia with Hungary. With the end of the First World War, Croatia joined Slovenia and Serbia in the new South Slavic state of Yugoslavia under the Serbian monarch (Herman, 1978:24).

The fifth and the present period begins, according to Herman (1978), with the creation of this new state in 1918. Karlovic, however, argues

> that this union was achieved arbitrarily... by force of arms, is suggested by the fact that an armed revolt in Croatia had to be quashed as early as the end of 1918. ...A campaign ... [presented] to the Allies in Versailles in 1919, with a request

for Croatia's independence, engendered widespread support, while a short-lived Croatian republic was proclaimed in 1919 (Karlovic, 1982:279).

This period was blemished by continued failures of the parliament to bring about a democratic form of government.

Croatians felt that they were extremely underrepresented in the parliamentary decision-making process. Furthermore, "the country was run essentially as a Greater Serbia, with Serbs controlling the political, military, administrative, and the financial system" (Karlovic, 1982:279). Finally, after Stjepan Radic, leader of the strongest Croatian party, was murdered in parliament by a Serbian (Montenegrin) representative in 1928, King Alexander (Serbian) abolished all democratic institutions and proclaimed himself a dictator (Herman, 1978:24).

With the German invasion of Yugoslavia in 1941, the Croatian union with Serbia came to a sudden end. Croatia, including the present day republic of Bosnia and Herzegovina, declared itself an independent state under the leadership of former Croatian exiles. Croats were once again divided. Some fought with the Germans in order to support the "independent state," while others fought with the leader of the partisan resistance, Josip Broz Tito, himself a Croatian.

The Croatian union with Serbia "was again re-established in 1945, this time under the aegis of Tito and the communist party" (Karlovic, 1982:279). Croatian nationalism in Yugoslavia continued to be evident in its struggle for democratization. Serbian hegemony in the fields of language, culture, economy, and the right to self-determination is something that Karlovic suggests will lead to continued instability:

> the promise or advent of economic parity need not lead to the demise of oppostiion in the periphery (Croatia), and it is probably a fallacy to expect that...even if economic equality with the dominant (Serbian) community is achieved. The desire to control one's political destiny would seem to override that....if the Croats were to profit in economic terms from their present situation, which they do not, this would hardly balance other political, cultural, and social disadvantages (1982:293).

He concludes:

> The frustration of the core (Serbian) community has been caused by its inability to achieve an even more dominant role, including the successful "Serbianization" of other peoples in that country, the Macedonians, Albanians, and Slovenes as well as the Croats. The frustration of the peripheral (Croatian) community results from Serbian exploitation (1982:294).

Specifically, Karlovic suggests: "the very nature of this relationship, which is likely to ensure the permanence of instability once the peripheral (Croatian) community has become conscious of its condition, and can expect such instability to continue in Yugoslavia" (1982:294).

While political turmoil continues to pl;ague the Balkan peninsula, Croatia, for the first time in modern history, has gained its independent status. Dr. Franjo Tudjman, leader of the Croatian Democratic Union and President of Croatia, proclaimed Croatian independence on 15 January 1992..

CROATIANS IN CANADA

Although it was noted that Croatians were among the first explorers of Canadian soil (two Croat sailors were members of Jacques Cartier's expedition in 1543), it was not until 1872 that an old seaman named Jure (George) left his Croatian sailing ship in Vancouver harbour to gain the first recorded privilege of a Croatian making Canada his new home (Paveskovic, 1970:480). It is also interesting to note that a Croatian sailor by the name of Kozulic visited the Canadian Pacific coast, thereby counting himself among the first explorers of British Columbia.

Croatian history, characterized by a struggle for cultural survival in Yugoslavia and abroad, is also characterized by mass emigration. Croatian emigrants numbered over one and one-half million or three-quarters of the total number of Yugoslavian nationalities (Holjevac, 1967:351). In his estimation (at the time of his book's publication) there were two million persons of Croatian origin living in Europe, North America, and South America (Holjevac, 1967:350).

Karlovic offers some more recent figures. Commenting on the export of labour, the number of Croatian migrant workers peaked in 1972 to 1.2

million. By 1979 it levelled off to somewhere around 860,000. Furthermore, "if one compared migration frequency strictly by ethnic group, regardless of the migrant's region of residence in the country, the imbalance is even clearer. Croats who also comprise the bulk of migrants from Bosnia and Herzegovina, are six times more likely to migrate than Serbs or Montenegrins" (Karlovic, 1982:285-286).

Rasporich, commenting on the emigration of Croats, writes: "the history of emigration is then the most intense of human dramas, which tells of those who through strength or weakness, fear or hope, boredom or adventure, decided to leave in search of a better life" (1979:11).

It is difficult to estimate the exact number of Croatians that arrived in Canada prior to World War I. However, some approximations estimate that between 1901 and 1911 there were slightly over 6000 from British Columbia to Quebec. The first settlements in Ontario were established in Welland in 1907, Schumacher in 1908, and Hamilton in 1910 (Paveskovic, 1970:481).

These first settlers did not conform to the stereotypical image of the Eastern European, a sheepskin clad peasant with a large family. Rather, the majority were single, highly mobile males in search of quick fortunes that they could bring back to their native villages in Croatia. In the late 1800s, many found prosperity as a result of the Alaskan Gold Rush. The abundance of salmon along the Pacific coast of British Columbia was a further incentive to a number of Croatian fisherman who were among the first to establish the British Columbia salmon fisheries (Rasporich, 1982:12-21).

The first wave of emigration to Canada, significantly smaller than the one to the United States, was prompted by an economic crisis in Croatia. It is estimated that over 30,000 Croatians emigrated to North America between 1880 and 1900. Rasporich proposes that "the desire for a better life ranked high in their aspirations, at least as high as the negative drives of poor land, excessive taxation, debt, and unemployment (1979, Chapter 2:13).

With the advent of World War I, many Croatians living in Canada feared political repercussions — they were considered subjects of the Austro-Hungarian monarchy — and fled to the United States. Consequently, immigration in Canada within the next few years came to a standstill.

The years of World War I, for Croatians in Canada, were characterized by an overwhelmingly negative reaction by Canadians, which by the end turned into hostility. The Canadian economy had to re-absorb a large number of veterans. As such, the returning soldier had a great deal of hostility towards those whom he perceived as enemy aliens who were competing for his job (Rasporich, 1982:41-48). "The Croats were in fact the Eastern European equivalent of the Japanese and East Indians who were met with hostility in the Port of Vancouver in 1907 and 1914" (Rasporich, 1982:48). Furthermore, they were considered a part of the German and Austrian collective — it was a time of stereotypical epithets such as "cowardly Huns" and "Prussian curs."

Between 1990 and 1920, the Croatian immigrant faced a cultural crisis as well as an identity crisis. Along with thousands of other Europeans, they settled onto the bottom rung of the social and economic ladder. As Rasporich (1982) points out, it was a time of drifting from one mine town to another in search of a job; family life was unknown. Furthermore,

> as peripheral entities in their day to day existence and cut off from their parent culture or its larger satellites in the United States, the Canadian Croats were exposed to a social melting pot....Insufficient in numbers to command any preferred status or to raise the necessary social capital for music, culture, or education, the community could only remain alive through informal means (Rasporich, 1979, Chapter 3:2).

Their tools for cultural survival were based on the traditional notions of peasant communal cooperation. In other words, when they emigrated they usually did so with their friends and relatives from their own villages.

The ensuing period between 1920 and 1930 was a decade of rapid growth for the Croatians. Changes in the Canadian immigration policy, combined with expansion in industry, opened the door for a new wave of Croatian immigrants. It is estimated that between 1920 and 1929 close to 11,000 Croatians entered Canada (Paveskovic, 1970:48).

This wave was once again predominantly male. The Canadian census, as quoted by Rasporich, shows that 73 per cent of Croatians in Canada were male. Demographically, in 1931, there was a total of 10,450 persons of Croatian origin living in Canada. Croats settled predominantly in the smaller urban centres, creating a 55 per cent urban versus 45 per cent rural split (Rasporich, 1982:94-98).

Approximately 6000 Croatians made Ontario their new home. The largest settlement was in Schumacher. There were over 400 Croats living in this town whose chief industry was mining. Without a church of their own, which is considered a bastion of ethnic tradition, Croats faced assimilation into the dominant English culture.

This was enhanced by the number of Croatian children entering the public school system. As Rasporich points out, in Schumacher "by 1930 the Croatian children had become a near deluge in virtually every grade, occasionally dominating a particular classroom" (1979, Chapter 5:29). That they maintained their traditions was illustrated by the formation of numerous cultural clubs.

The first Croatian settlement in Toronto comprised approximately 400 individuals and was established in the southwest part of the city around 1925. Still, they were submerged within a larger urban community (Rasporich, 1979:38-40). Relying primarily on manual labour for employment, they believed in the value of education, subscribing to a native saying that "a people without education are a people without a future."

The educational philosophy of the time was succinctly stated by Rasporich: "they [Croatians] were thus prepared to consign their young children fully and unreservedly to the urban school system of their adopted country, and not yet endure the cult of illiteracy that became popular among future generations of Canadian born adolescents" (1979, Chapter 5:52). Therefore, it is interesting to note that Croatians did not exhibit the educational aspiration traits of agrarian-based migratory collectives. Although the parents often had no formal education themselves, they inculcated the importance of education to their children.

The decade of the 1920s proved to be fruitful, both in human and material terms. Croats were optimistic: "the old, because they and their children had shed the bitter memories of wartime persecution as aliens, and the new, because they had barely escaped the tentacles of rural poverty in the developing dictatorship of King Alexander's Yugoslavia" (Rasporich, 1979, Chapter 5:81).

Between 1930 and 1940, an acceleration towards integration into the Canadian way of life took place. The inclination to do so was enhanced by the stock market crash and the ensuing Depression. Moreover, Stephen Leacock seemed to have recanted on his racist philosophy towards European immigrants, which was stated in a speech in 1936:

> I met a fellow from Europe the other day — a Croat... or something. Where was it he said he came from? Toschen or Poschen, anyway, somewhere. And he seemed alright, a nice little "feller." How often do you hear people say, "I couldn't see anything wrong with them." ... All things we value they value (Rasporich, 1979, Chapter 6:22-23).

Thereby Croatians were shedding the previous stereotype that they were "an unassimilable radical lump in the national digestive track" (Rasporich, 1979, Chapter 6:23). With the maturing of the first Canadian-born Croatian generation and a lack of Croatian brides there was a high rate of exogamous marriage. Although intermarriages occurred between Slavic collectives, about one-third of all marriages in the group were to people of British stock (Rasporich, 1979, Chapter 6:25).

Biographically, Croats of the time were represented in a colourful fashion. Louis Adamic, a Slovenian living in America, wrote:

> The Croats are real peasants, slow, plodding persevering; sad, idealistic, naive, muddled, tragic-minded, not easily articulate, superstitious; always complaining, but in the curious mingling of pagan and Catholic faiths, with their constitutional distrust of everything not of their making, infinitely patient and quietly strong — in brief full of positive and negative traits (Rasporich, 1982:4).

The climate of the 1930s was, however, split into two ideologies — the "melting pot" and the "multicultural mosaic." Croatians were divided on the issues as they related to notions of integration. Publicly they were most interested in adopting their new country's way of life. At home they stuck to their native traditions, which were strongly ingrained in their religious upbringing.

The outbreak of World War II gave Croatians a chance to further shed the image of alliance with the Austro-Hungarian empire of World War I. They were united in their allegiance to crush any sort of totalitarian regime. An editorial in *Hrvatski Glas*, a Croatian newspaper in Canada, called on Croats to "crush Nazism, Fascism, Communism, and all subversive elements which are attempting to undermine and overthrow our government by force and violence" (Rasporich, 1979, Chapter 6:50). In essence, the decade ended with a great number of Canadian-born Croatians assimilating into Canadian society.

The period between 1940 and 1955 was, among Croatians, characterized by the shifting allegiance of Croats to Josip Broz and the Partisans, and Dr. Ante Pavelic, president of the short-lived independent state of Croatia. Nevertheless, it was estimated that by 1959 close to 20,000 Yugoslavian refugees had entered Canada. The lack of more detailed information makes it difficult to estimate how many of those were Croatian.

The economic climate in Canada was conducive to the absorption of these new immigrants, who at this time were not composed of the peasant, semi-literate, agrarian population of earlier decades, but rather of a large number of professionals, priests, and intellectuals. They were motivated to leave their homeland as a result of ideological differences. Once settled in the new country they worked in manual labour camps in the remote areas of the Canadian frontier. It is estimated that five per cent of workers in these camps were of Croatian origin (Rasporich, 1979, Chapter 7:34).

These new immigrants, nevertheless, faced a great deal of alienation. Integration onto the Canadian mainstream was difficult. Language skills, traditions and values overemphasized their Croatian past.

As a result, cleavages between pre-war generations of Croatian-Canadians and postwar ones deepened both politically and socially. The new generation was interested in financial success precluded by the perceived oppression by the dominant ruling class. The immigrant of the 1920s, was happy in the acquisition of a new home provided by hard work. Thus, the Canadian way of life was favoured (Rasporich, 1979, Chapter 7:39-41).

The climate of the times was not conducive to the development of high educational aspirations in the Croatian collective. This was especially evident in the growing shift between the old and the new generation. *Zajednicar*, a Croatian weekly newspaper printed in the United States, illustrates that although by the 1940s and early 1950s there were over 400,000 Croatians, there were only 135 identified college students (Bodnar, 1976:9).

This is not to say that there were no intellectuals who tried to inculcate higher aspirations into the Croatian masses. Francis Preveden, a leading Croatian intellectual in the early 1940s, constantly expounded the philosophy that Croatians should strive towards vertical mobility through the channels of higher education. The reaction of Croats in the United States was that they were not willing to give in to American middle-class values, which tended to emphasize mobility through education (Boadar, 1976:9).

The philosophy of Croatians in Canada differs from that of Croato-Americans. Rasporich (1979) claimed that there was an influx of middle-class, urban-based Croat immigrants in the period between 1946 and 1955. He states that social aspirations of this collective reflected the North American values of mobility through education; in other words, "two children, a home, a car, and steady employment" (1979, Chapter 8:2). However, Holjevac pointed out that during the same period Croatians in

Canada were strongly overrepresented in predominantly blue-collar mining positions (1967:156).

Neither author offers a clear picture of the extent of educational aspirations at the time. Rasporich (1979) points to the parental wishes for "two educated children," however, he does not state whether these aspirations were to continue past compulsory education. Holjevac (1967), commenting on the occupational overrepresentation in blue-collar positions, hints at the lack of vertical mobility. However, he does not explain to what extent, if any, Croats aspired towards better education and, consequently, greater upward mobility.

Herman (1978) in his Ph.D. thesis "Comparative Analysis of the Occupational Choices of Croatians in Ontario," while dealing with the subject in an anthropological framework, writes one sentence on educational aspirations. He proposed that Croatian families living in Ontario in the early 1950s had high aspirations for their children. This response was interpreted in a manner that suggested that parents would be happy if their children landed some sort of government job. Unfortunately, no other elaboration is provided.

The period between 1955 and 1975 saw the largest influx of Croatian immigrants into Canada. Out of approximately 70,000, it is estimated that 20,000 were classified as refugees. Close to 72 per cent settled in Ontario, with over 40,000 in Toronto and vicinity (Rasporich, 1979, Chapter 8:16-118).

Croatian population in Canada, according to the 1981 census based on a 20 per cent sample data, comprised 34,765 identified Croatians, of which the largest aggregate, 26,640, made Ontario their home. Interestingly, the population of Yugoslavs (not otherwise stated) for Canada amounted to 64,835. For Ontario the respective figure was 41,435 (Statistics Canada, 1981 Census of Canada; Cat. 92911).

It is difficult to suggest the reason for such a large number of Yugoslavs (not otherwise stated). However, if we take Holjevac's (1967) suggestion that of all Yugoslav nationalities emigrating to Canada and elsewhere three-quarters were Croatian, we can suggest that three-quarters of those Yugoslavs, not otherwise stated, are Croatian. Thus for the 1981 census, Croatian population in Canada can be estimated at 83,392. For Ontario the figure would be 55,717.

Part of the migration movement in the late 1950s and 1960s saw the majority of foreign-born Croatians employed in construction and secondary manufacturing. This population accounted for 50 per cent of the total workforce in Canada (Rasporich, 1979, Chapter 8:18-20). Canadian-born, second generation Croats fared much better; nine per cent were members of the manufacturing and construction workforce. This group, according to Rasporich, was heavily concentrated in pursuit of white-collar and professional occupations (Rasporich, 1979, Chapter 8:19).

This diversity in occupational hierarchy between the newly arrived immigrants and the already settled Croatian Canadians most likely created a deepening cleavage in the perception of social and economic mobility. The foreign-born Croatian immigrants, who were educated and urban-based, were probably far more jaded in their perceptions of the Candian opportunity structure then were their Canadian-born counterparts.

However, some of these problems were soon to be alleviated, since the sheer number of new immigrants would allow for the establishment of social and cultural centres. One of the first formal institutions, central to all Toronto Croatians, was a Roman Catholic church completed in 1965, "Our Lady Queen of Croatia," located on the recently renamed Croatia Street in the Bloor and Dufferin area. The area became the focus of Croatian residency. Specifically, a large concentration of Croatian families moved into the area bounded by Yonge Street to the east, Keele Street to the west, Lawrence Avenue to the north, and Lakeshore Boulevard to the south.

Although Our Lady Queen of Croatia played an important role in the community structure, it did not give rise to a distinct Croatian-Catholic culture. As Msgr. Stankovic, observing from Rome, remarked: "sociological divisions within three generations of Croatian immigrants militated against the formation of a Croatian ethnic Catholic community" (Rasporich, 1979, Chapter 8:26).

With an expanding number of Croatians living in Toronto, there came an expanding number of ethnic halls as well as culturally oriented and politically motivated halls. Moreover, Croatians fielded teams in many sports. For example, "Croatia Soccer Club" was a predecessor to the famous "Metros-Croatia," winner of the 1976 North American Soccer Championship.

Hence, the 1960s and 1970s produced a different type of Croatian immigrant. The political climate of the time allowed this better-educated class of Croatian immigrants a chance to uphold and preserve the old culture and explore the avenues of the new. As Rasporich elaborates: "The position of the postwar emigres... was thus one of dual allegiance to two cultures, languages and life styles — the preservation of the old and cautious adoption of the new" (1979, Chapter 8:32).

Certainly, one of the most important institutions in the preservation of cultural-ethnic heritage is the family. The Croatian family may, in the broader context, be described as a patriarchal one. The basic premise of each family is the same as that of its historical counterpart. They value hard work, thus reflecting an aspiration towards upward social mobility. As was the case with the previous generation, the Croatian family of the 1970s inculcated high educational aspirations into their children as a way of upward social mobility.

SUMMARY

Maintenance of ethnic identity among Croatians has historically been very important. Resulting from the sudden exploration of the "roots syndrome," many second and third generation Croatians find themselves returning to the cultural traditions of their forefathers. Rasporich suggests that these children will always carry with them ways of thinking and feeling that are unique to Croatian Canadians (1979, Chapter 8:74). Given the opportunity, like their Croatian ancestors, Canadian-Croatians they would make a mark upon Canadian history.

CHAPTER FOUR

Study Methodology

The focus of this study is an examination of a select number of variables associated with educational aspirations. The general hypothesis is that, despite background limitations, Croatian youth in Toronto high schools will have fairly high aspirations, because immigrant families in the Canadian context are highly motivated to achieve success for themselves and even more so for their children.

Explicitly, the hypotheses of this study are concerned with such independent variables as socio-economic origin, gender, peer influence, self-concept, perception of opportunity, parental influence, religious origin, and regional origin. Socio-economic origin variables included father's education, mother's education, father's occupation, mother's occupation, and family income. The dependent variable in the study is educational aspirations.

The study's population consisted of Croatian high school students in Toronto and vicinity. As it was difficult to arrive at a random sample of Croatian youth, we relied on a purposive sample. We approached a number of voluntary Croatian youth organizations, including Croatian students attending Croatian heritage language classes, church youth groups, and Croatian folklore and tambouritza (a stringed instrument similar to a mandolin)ensembles.

As such our sample may not necessarily be representative of Croatian high school students in general. However, they could be characterized as "Croato-centric," that is, a group of strong, culturally bound Croatian youth.

The Sample

Subjects consisted of 127 students of Croatian origin living within the greater Toronto area. For the purposes of this study, Croatian origin is defined as those subjects who were either born in Croatia or whose father or mother, or both, were born in Croatia. Thus, all of the subjects in this study were either first or second generation Croatians. Of these, 46 were males, 76 were females, and 5 did not identify their gender. Subjects were registered in grades 9 through 12 on a full-time basis at various high schools in the greater Toronto area. Of the total number of subjects who participated in this study, 44 were registered in grade 9, 37 in grade 10, 16 in grade 11, and 24 in grade 12. Of the 127 subjects, 104 attended Catholic high schools, 18 attended public schools and 5 did not identify their school origin.

Since it is very difficult to do research on ethnicity in Toronto due to the lack of information available from most school boards, the present study employed the "purposive sample" technique to recruit its subjects. Such a method allows the researcher the opportunity to develop an ever-increasing set of observations through the recommendation of other subjects by the present participants.

As mentioned, the researcher obtained the initial participants from various Croatian social and educational groups and clubs. Other subjects were recommended by the participants of these clubs. In all, 127 were appropriate respondents.

The questionnaires were distributed on a number of appropriate occasions (such as club gatherings, dance practices, and language classes). On each occasion the researcher was present to distribute and collect the questionnaires and answer any queries pertinent to question clarification.

Research Design

The questionnaire contained questions primarily concerned with educational aspirations and expectations, socio-economic origin, perception of peer influence, opinions on self-concept, perception of opportunity, parental influence, and finally, background information concerned with gender, regional origin, and religious origin.

The format of the questionnaire was fairly structured to facilitate accuracy as well as to ensure that most were completed within a 30 to 40 minute time span. Questions were constructed by drawing upon questionnaires employed in previous research (Anisef et al., 1980; Calliste, 1980; Porter et al., 1982) so that some sort of equivalence could be maintained between the present study and past Canadian research. This task was undertaken strictly for comparative purposes.

OPERATIONALIZATION OF VARIABLES

Dependent Variable

For the present study, the dependent variable is educational aspirations. This variable was measured by asking students two questions related to this theme:

(1) When would you prefer to leave high school?
The three response categories for this question were: grade 12; grade 13; or other, please write in. This question was directly followed by:

(2) Then what would you like to do?
The possible responses were: work full-time; go into apprenticeship or to a private commercial, business, or trade school; go to community college; go to university, but probably not graduate; graduate from university; do further studies at university after graduating from university; study part-time at a university or community college while working either full-time or part-time; other, please describe; or I don't know.

The category responses for this second question are in an ascending order (working full-time was given the lowest value, and doing "post-graduate university work" was given the highest value) in order to obtain a greater measure of aspirations. The researcher feels that providing students with categories ensures more specific and mutually exclusive responses.

These response categories were used in cross-tabular examinations frequently collapsing them into two categories: those aspiring to attend university and those not wishing to attend university. These transformations were conducted since there was a large number of students aspiring towards a university education or higher. Finally, these response categories were treated as interval scales for the purpose of regression analysis.

Independent Variables

The independent variables for this present study were developed on the basis of pertinent literature review and were grouped into five groups. Once again they were socio-economic origin, significant other variable, self-concept and perception of ability, demographic variables, and school variables.

Socio-economic Origin

The social origins of the students were determined using various measures related to parental educational and occupational attainments. The fathers' and mothers' education was measured by asking the students, "How far did your parents or guardians go in school? Indicate the highest level of schooling each has."

The response categories for both parents were: none; completed grade 4; completed grade 8; some high or secondary school; business or technical school; attended university or college but did not graduate; graduated from university; did further study at university after graduation from university; or other, please write in. Again, the categories were listed in an ascending order to ensure greater specificity.

The responses were collapsed into a three-level ordinal scale: grade 4 or less; grade 5 through 8; higher than grade 8. The reasons these categories were collapsed is because only 7.1 per cent of the fathers had some university or college and only 5.5 per cent had completed university or engaged in postgraduate studies. Comparative figures for mothers are 4.7 per cent attended university or college and did not graduate, whereas, 3.2 per cent graduated from university or did postgraduate work. The percentage of fathers and mothers that had less than grade 8 was 44.9 and 49.6, respectively.

Mothers' occupations were measured by asking students: "What is your mother's or female guardian's job or occupation? Be as specific as you can. Tell us not only what she does but what sort of place she works in. For instance, she is a nursing aide in a nursing home; she is a university professor; she cleans in a hospital; she is a keypunch operator in a bank; she sews dresses in a small factory." The responses were open-ended even though examples were provided.

Mothers' occupations were ranked on the Pineo-Porter (1967) Prestige Scale and collapsed into two nominal categories: unskilled and skilled. Unskilled occupations included farmers or labourers, unskilled manual, unskilled clerical and sales, and semi-skilled manual. The skilled professions included those involved in semi-skilled clerical and sales, farmers, skilled crafts, skilled clerical and sales, foremen, supervisors, middle managers, technicians, semi-professionals, high-level managers, employed professionals, self-employed professionals.

Fathers' occupations were measured in a similar fashion. Students were asked: "What is your father's or male guardian's job or occupation outside the home? If he works on more than one job, put down the one in which he spends the most time. If he is unemployed or has retired, put down what he used to do. Be as specific as you can. Tell us not only what he does but what sort of place he works in. For instance, he operates a punch press in a metal shop; he is an attendant in a hospital; he drives a truck for a small company; he is a university student."

Again, the responses were open-ended even though examples were provided. The responses were similarly ranked on the Pineo-Porter (1967) Prestige Scale and further collapsed into two nominal categories: unskilled and skilled (Table 3A). The occupations included in each of these categories were identical to the mothers' occupations.

The students' economic origins were determined by inquiring about family income. Subjects were asked: "To the best of your knowledge, what was your parents' total income before taxes in the past year?" Response categories varied from "under $25,000" to "$75,001 and over." Response categories were collapsed into a three-level ordinal scale: less than $35,000; $35,001 to $60,000; $60,000 or more.

Significant Other Variables

The influence of parents, peers, and teachers on the aspirations of students was measured by asking: "In general, to what extent have each of the following people encouraged or discouraged you to continue your education after high school? Circle only one number for each person." The possible answers were: mother, father; sisters and/or brothers; other relatives; friends in colleges; friends in universities; other friends; your boyfriend or girlfriend; teachers; guidance counsellors; or other, specify.

Students were asked to describe the degree of encouragement or lack thereof on a scale from "discouraged you very much" to "encouraged you very much," or "not applicable." From these responses the researcher was able to arrive at a better understanding of the importance of peers and parental influence on aspirations.

Self-concept and Perception of Ability

Self-concept was measured by asking students several questions related to their perceptions of their scholastic ability. Students were asked how they rate themselves in school ability compared with close friends and classmates. The response categories employed the Self-concept of Ability Scale originally used by Brookover (1963) and modified by Calliste (1980). The following are examples of the possible responses: well above average; somewhat above average; average; somewhat below average; or well below average.

These response categories were used in ordinal scales in a cross-tabular analysis, usually collapsing them into three categories: average or below; somewhat above average; or well above average. These transformations were conducted since there were only a few students in the other categories.

Students were also asked whether they think they have the academic ability to graduate from university, and how likely they think it is that they would study beyond the undergraduate level. Again, the response categories employed Calliste's (1980) modified Self-concept of Ability Scale. Examples of the response categories include: very likely; somewhat likely; not sure either way; unlikely; or most unlikely. Again, a collapsing of these responses was necessary since the number of students in most categories was quite small. Therefore, for cross-tabular analysis, the responses were collapsed into three categories: not sure; probably; or definitely.

Demographic Variables

Sex, birth order, number of siblings, country of birth, and place of residence were all measured by straightforward questions.

Gender was measured by asking the students, "What is your sex?" Response categories were: male; or female.

Birth order and number of siblings was established by first asking: "Among your parents' children, are you the: first born; second born; third born; fourth born; fifth born; sixth born, or born later than sixth." The responses were again collapsed due to the low number of students born fourth in line or higher. The collapsed response categories were: first born; second born; third born or higher.

The students' as well as their parents' birthplaces were determined using a straightforward question: "In what country were you and your parents born? Circle one number for yourself and each parent." The possible responses were: Canada; Croatia; other country, please write in. Since all the respondents were ether born in Croatia or Canada, the third category was eliminated in the cross-tabular analysis of this variable.

The last demographic variable, "place of residence," was ascertained by inquiring: "How would you describe the place where you lived for the longest time? Circle one number." The possible responses were: in a city; in a small town; in a village or a small community; other, please describe. Although these categories were quite exhaustive, the majority of the respondents resided in a city for most of their lives, thus for the purposes of cross-tabular anlaysis the reponse categories were collapsed to: city; or other.

School Variables

Since the educational system plays an important role in the educational aspirations of students, our analysis of school variables was a crucial component of this present study. The variables that were measured were grade level of students, type of school attended, and, most importantly, grades received.

The grade level of students was discovered by simply asking: "What grade are you in?" Since the present study used high school students, the only possible responses were: grade 9; grade 10; grade 11; grade 12.

The type of school attended was also determined in a very basic and straightforward fashion. Subjects were asked: "Are you presently attending: Catholic high school; public high school; or other, please specify." All subjects were either attending a Catholic or a public high school, therefore, the response categories were collapsed to the aforementioned two.

The last school variable, grades received, is the most important since it denotes how well the student has mastered the subject matter of his or her courses. Unfortunately, the researcher of the present study was limited by time and money and consequently was unable to administer a standardized achievement test. As a result, the grades reported by students may have been somewhat subjective. Nevertheless, students were asked, "What were most of your grades or marks last year, or the last year you were in school?"

The possible response categories were: mostly 80 per cent and over; mostly 70-79 per cent; mostly 60-69 per cent; mostly 50-59 per cent; mostly under 50 per cent; or other, explain. Last year's grades were analyzed since they were more concrete than an abstract explanation of this year's grades. A fair collapsing of the response categories for the purpose of cross-tabular analysis resulted in three response categories: less than 60 per cent; 70-79 per cent; or 80 per cent or above. In essence, the researcher measured whether the respondent was a "C," "B," or "A" student, and the effects of these grades on "educational aspirations."

DATA ANALYSIS

The first method of analysis was cross-tabular analysis. By using this method the researcher was able to independently examine the effects of a number of independent variables on the dependent variable, "educational aspirations." The contingency tables describe the associations among the various categories of the independent and dependent variables, both in the original form and also in the collapsed category format. The Chi-square (X^2) is computed for every cross-tabular analysis. The association is significant if the P-value is less than .05, and it approaches significance if the P-value is less than .10. The gamma is computed for ordinal or ratio variables, and the Cramer's V, or phi is computed for nominal variables.

The second and final method of analysis was the multiple regression analysis of the dependent variable on the basis of the values of the independent variables. For the purposes of this analysis, the betas were computed. Betas measure the influence that independent variables have on dependent variables, that is, how much "Y" increases if "X" is increased for one unit, and all other predictors remain the same. As well, as further measure of association, the R-square and Adj. R-square were computed.

SUMMARY

As the literature has shown, the educational aspiration-formation process for adolescents is characterized by a number of influences. The aforementioned type of anlyasis is best suited to test the effects of these variables and their influences on this particular sample of Croatian youth and their educational aspirations.

CHAPTER FIVE

Results

Based on our review of the pertinent literature and our own information on the background characteristics of Croatians living in Toronto and vicinity, we feel that the following hypotheses are most relevant to Croatian youths' educational aspiration-formation processes.

TESTS OF HYPOTHESES

Hypothesis 1

> Among Croatian young people, the father's education does not have an effect on educational aspirations.

What Table 1 suggests is that there is no relationship between the father's education and the subject's aspirations. Forty-two per cent of subjects whose fathers had less than a grade 4 education aspired towards university education. Thirty-two per cent aspired towards an education higher than a B.A.

Similarly, subjects whose fathers had five to eight years of schooling aspired towards a B.A. (69 per cent) and higher than a B.A. (4 per cent).

TABLE 1
Aspirations by Father's Education

Aspirations	Father's Education		
	Grade 4 or less	Grade 5-8	Higher than Grade 8
No University	26	27	20
B.A.	42	69	60
Higher than B.A.	32	4	20
Total Per Cent	100	100	100
Number	31	26	64

Total N 121
Missing Observations 6
Chi-square = 8.23,
   d.f. = 4, n.s.
Gamma = 0.01

Finally, subjects whose fathers had completed more than eight years of formal education aspired towards a B.A. (60 per cent) and higher than a B.A. (20 per cent). Table 1 shows that the father's education does not have a significant effect on educational aspirations. The Chi-square was found to be 8.23 (df = 4, p<.10). It is, however, important to note that although this result is not significant, the Chi-square does approach significance. Gamma, used to measure direction as well as magnitude of association, was found to be 0.01. The data (Table 1) support the hypothesis that there is no association between the father's education and the subject's aspirations, therefore, it may be accepted.

Consequently, as a result of a large number of respondents aspiring towards a university education or higher, we decided to find out the effects of the father's education on just two groups of subjects' aspirations: those aspiring to attend university and those not wishing to attend university.

Table 1A shows that 74 per cent of subjects whose fathers have less than a grade 4 education aspire towards a university degree. Seventy-three per cent of subjects whose fathers have a grade 5 to 8 education aspire towards a university education, and finally, 80 per cent of subjects whose

RESULTS

TABLE 1A
Aspirations by Father's Education

Aspirations	Father's Education		
	Grade 4 or less	Grade 5-8	Higher than Grade 8
No University	26	27	20
University	74	73	80
Total Per Cent	100	100	100
Number	31	26	64
Total N	121		
Missing Observations	6		

Chi-square = 0.62,
   d.f. = 2, n.s.
Gamma = 0.13

fathers have completed more than eight years of formal education aspire towards a university degree.

Thus, in collapsing the categories, we have shown that the father's education does not have a significant impact on the subject's aspirations. Table 1A shows that the Chi-square for the father's education was found to be .62 (df = 2, n.s.). Similarly, no association was observed in the gamma measure (gamma = .13).

Once again, the data in Table 1A confirm that there is no association between fathers' education and subjects' aspirations, therefore, our hypothesis may be accepted.

Hypothesis 2

> Among Croatian young people, the mother's education does not have an effect on educational aspirations.

Table 2 reveals that there is no relationship between the mother's education and the subject's aspirations.

TABLE 2
Aspirations by Mother's Education

	Mother's Education		
Aspirations	Grade 4 or less	Grade 5-8	Higher than Grade 8
No University	25	36	16
B.A.	58	52	58
Higher than B.A.	17	12	26
Total Per Cent	100	100	100
Number	40	25	57
Total N	122		
Missing Observations	5		
Chi-square = 5.32, d.f. = 4, n.s.			
Gamma = 0.21			

Fifty-eight per cent of subjects whose mothers have less than a grade 4 education aspired towards university, whereas 17 per cent aspired towards an education higher than a B.A. Fifty-two per cent of subjects whose mothers have five to eight years of schooling aspire towards a B.A., whereas 12 per cent aspire towards an education higher than a B.A.

Finally, 58 per cent of subjects whose mothers have completed more than eight years of formal education aspire towards a B.A., and 26 per cent aspire towards an education higher than a B.A.

Table 2 shows that the mother's education does not have a significant effect on educational aspirations. The Chi-square for the mother's education was found to be 5.32 (df = 4, n.s.). A further test of association also reveals no relationship (gamma = 0.21).

The data (Table 2) support the hypothesis that there is no association between mothers' education and subjects' aspirations, therefore it may be accepted.

RESULTS

TABLE 3
Aspirations by Father's Occupation

Aspirations	Father's Occupation			
	Unskilled	Semi-skilled	Middle Managers	Professionals
No University	29	14	31	28
B.A.	52	65	54	43
Higher than B.A.	19	21	15	29
Total Per Cent	100	100	100	100
Number	48	48	13	7
Total N	116			
Missing Observations	11			
Chi-square = 4.08, d.f. = 6, n.s.				
Gamma = 0.07				

Unskilled: includes farmers or labourers, unskilled manual, unskilled clerical and sales, semi-skilled manual.

Semi-Skilled: includes semi-skilled clerical and sales, farmers, skilled crafts, skilled clerical and sales.

Middle Managers: includes formen, supervisors, middle managers, technicians.

Professionals: includes semi-professionals, high-level managers, employed professionals, self-employed professionals.

Hypothesis 3

Among Croatian young people, the father's occupation does not have an effect on educational aspirations.

The Cats-Pineo-Porter Scale provided us with the categories for the father's occupation. Table 3 shows that 52 per cent of subjects whose fathers are categorized as "unskilled" aspire towards a university degree, whereas 19 per cent of subjects whose fathers fit the same category aspire

TABLE 3A
Aspirations by Father's Occupation

	Father's Occupation	
Aspirations	Unskilled	Skilled
No University	29	19
University	71	81
Total Per Cent	100	100
Number	48	68
Total N	116	
Missing Observations	11	
Chi-square = 1.08, d.f. = 1, n.s.		
Gamma = 0.27		

Unskilled: includes farmers or labourers, unskilled manual, unskilled clerical and sales, semi-skilled manual.

Skilled: includes semi-skilled clerical and sales, farmers, skilled crafts, skilled clerical and sales, foremen, supervisors, middle managers, technicians, semi-professionals, high-level managers, employed professionals, self-employed professionals.

towards an education higher than a B.A. Sixty-five per cent of subjects whose fathers are categorized as "semi-skilled" aspire towards a university education, whereas 21 per cent of subjects whose fathers belong to the same category aspire towards an education higher than a B.A. Fifty-four per cent of subjects whose fathers are categorized in "middle management" positions aspire towards a university degree, whereas 15 per cent of subjects whose fathers fit the same category aspire towards an education greater than a B.A. Finally, 43 per cent of subjects whose fathers' occupations are "professional" aspire towards a university education, whereas 29 per cent of subjects whose fathers fit the same category aspire towards a "higher than B.A." education.

RESULTS

Table 3 suggests that the father's occupation does not have a significant effect on educational aspirations. The Chi-square for the father's occupation is 4.08 (df = 6, n.s.), gamma = 0.07. The data (Table 3) support the hypothesis that there is no association between fathers' occupations and subjects' aspirations. Therefore, it may be accepted.

Consequently, as a result of a small number of respondents' fathers belonging in the professional to semi-skilled categories, we decided to study the effects of just two types of categories of fathers' occupations ("unskilled" and "skilled") on two categories of subjects' aspirations ("non-university" and "university").

Table 3A reveals that 71 per cent of subjects whose fathers are in the "unskilled" category aspire towards a university degree, whereas 81 per cent of subjects whose fathers are in the "skilled" category aspire towards a university degree.

Thus, in collapsing the categories, we have shown that fathers' occupation does not have a significant impact on subjects' aspirations. Table 3A shows that the Chi-square is 1.08 (df = 1, n.s.). Similarly, a weak association was observed in the gamma measure (gamma = 0.27).

Once again, the data in Table 3A confirm that there is no association between fathers' occupations and subjects' aspirations, therefore, our hypothesis may be accepted.

Hypothesis 4

> Among Croatian young people, the mother's occupation does not have an effect on educational aspirations.

Since there was found to be a small number of respondents' mothers in the professional (n = 1) to semi-skilled (n = 2) categories, Table 4 will discuss the above-mentioned hypothesis with reference to two types of categories of mothers' occupations ("unskilled" and "skilled"), and three categories of subjects' aspirations ("no university", "B.A.", and "higher than B.A.").

Once again, the Cats-Pineo-Porter Scale provided us with the categories for mothers' occupations.

Table 4 suggests that 56 per cent of subjects whose mothers are categorized as "unskilled" aspire towards a university degree, whereas 15 per cent of those whose mothers fit the same category aspire towards an

TABLE 4
Aspirations by Mother's Occupation

Aspirations	Mother's Occupation	
	Unskilled	Skilled
No University	29	10
B.A.	56	58
Higher than B.A.	15	32
Total Per Cent	100	100
Number	52	31
Total N	83	
Missing Observations	44	
Chi-square = 5.86, d.f. = 2 p<.10	(approaches significance)	
Gamma = 0.47		

Unskilled: includes farmers or labourers, unskilled manual, unskilled clerical and sales, semi-skilled manual.

Skilled: includes semi-skilled clerical and sales, farmers, skilled crafts, skilled clerical and sales, foremen, supervisors, middle managers, technicians, semi-professionals, high-level managers, employed professionals, self-employed professionals.

education higher than a B.A. Fifty-eight per cent of subjects whose mothers are categorized as "skilled" aspire towards a university degree, whereas 32 per cent of subjects whose mothers fit the same category aspire towards an education higher than a B.A.

Table 4 shows that the mother's occupation does not have a significant effect on educational aspirations. The Chi-square for mother's occupation is 5.86 (df = 2, p<.10), gamma = 0.47. The data (Table 4) support the hypothesis that there is no association between mothers' occupations and subjects' aspirations. However, the Chi-square approaches significance, therefore, one may suggest a very limited significance. As well, the gamma value shows some association.

TABLE 5
Aspirations by Family Income

Aspirations	Family Income		
	Less than $35,000	$35,001-$60,000	Greater than $60,000
No University	8	38	19
B.A.	73	48	57
Higher than B.A.	19	14	24
Total Per Cent	100	100	100
Number	26	42	37
Total N	105		
Missing Observations	22		

Chi-square = 9.67,
d.f. = 4, p<0.05
Gamma = -0.004

Hypothesis 5

> Among Croatian young people, family income does not have an effect on educational aspirations.

Table 5 suggests that there is a relationship between family incomes and subjects' educational aspirations. Among those respondents whose family income is less than $35,000 per year, 73 per cent aspire towards a university education, whereas 19 per cent aspire towards an education higher than a B.A. Among those subjects whose family income range from $35,001 to $60,000 per year, 48 per cent aspire towards a university degree, whereas 14 per cent aspire towards an education higher than a B.A. Finally, among those respondents whose family income is greater than $60,000 per year, 57 per cent aspire towards a university degree, whereas 24 per cent aspire towards an education higher than a B.A.

Table 5 reveals that family income does have a significant effect on educational aspirations. The Chi-square for family income was found to be

9.67 (df = 4, p. < .05). However, the gamma statistic was found to be -.004, which implies no association. This is due to the curvilinear relationship that exists between income and educational aspirations. The reader should note the apparent inconsistency between Table 5 and Table 3 (Aspirations by Family Income and Aspirations by Father's Occupation, respectively). It would seem that the most ambitious in terms of father's occupation are those in the semi-skilled category; and the least ambitious in terms of income are those in the middle managers category. We propose that such an inconsistency is due to the fact that those in the central category view education as more important and, as such, do not yet have the skepticism of those subjects belonging to the higher socio-economic strata. It should be noted that these results do not support the conventional hypothesis that aspirations rise as socio-economic status rises.

However, the data (Table 5) do not support the hypothesis that there is no association between family income and subjects' educational aspirations. Therefore, the above mentioned hypothesis should be rejected.

Hypothesis 6

> Among Croatian young people, gender does not have an effect on educational aspirations.

Table 6 suggests that a relationship exists between gender and subjects' educational aspirations. Among the males of the sample, 63 per cent aspire towards a university degree and 7 per cent aspire towards an education greater than a B.A. Among the females of the sample, 53 per cent aspire towards a university degree and 29 per cent aspire towards an education greater than a B.A.

Thus, Table 6 shows that gender does have a significant effect on educational aspirations since the Chi-square was found to be 9.38 (df = 2, p < .01); the Cramer's V = 0.28, implying a weak association. The higher proportion of females aspiring towards university completion could be the result of a greater number of females in our sample. Again, it should be noted that the data go against the conventional findings that a higher proportion of males aspire towards university completion.

RESULTS

TABLE 6
Aspirations by Gender

Aspirations	Gender	
	Male	Female
No University	30	18
B.A.	63	53
Higher than B.A.	7	29
Total Per Cent	100	100
Number	46	76
Total N	122	
Missing Observations	5	
Chi-square = 9.38, d.f. = 2 $p<0.01$ Cramer's V = 0.28		

The data (Table 6) do not support the hypothesis of no association between gender and educational aspirations. Therefore, the hypothesis should be rejected.

Hypothesis 7

> Among Croatian young people, grade level does not have an effect on educational aspirations.

Since there was a small number of respondents in the higher levels of grade 11 (n = 3) and grade 12 (n = 3) aspiring towards a higher than B.A. education, Table 7 will discuss the above-mentioned hypothesis with reference to two types of educational aspirations categories: "university" and "non-university" aspirations.

TABLE 7
Aspirations by Grade Level

Aspirations	Grade 9	Grade 10	Grade 11	Grade 12
No University	20	16	19	42
University	80	84	81	58
Total Per Cent	100	100	100	100
Number	44	37	16	24
Total N	121			
Missing Observations	6			

Chi-square = 5.98,
 d.f. = 3, n.s.
Gamma = -0.25

Table 7 shows that 80 per cent of respondents from the grade 9 level aspire towards a university education, 84 per cent from the grade 10 level aspire towards a university education, 81 per cent of subjects belonging to the grade 11 level aspire towards a university degree, and, finally, 58 per cent of respondents enrolled in grade 12 aspire towards a university education.

Table 7 indicates that grade level does not have a significant effect on educational aspirations. The Chi-square for grade level was observed to be 5.98 (df = 3, n.s.). Similarly, the gamma measure (-0.25) of association also reveals a weak relationship between grade level and educational aspirations. The fact that the gamma is negative suggests that as the grade level increases aspirations decrease, particularly for the grade 12 cohort. We suggest that students at this grade level are simply more realistic about their educational attainment potential and as such align their aspirations closer to their educational abilities.

However, the data (Table 7) support the hypothesis that there is no association between the grade level of respondents and their educational aspirations. Therefore, this hypothesis may be accepted.

RESULTS

TABLE 8
Aspirations by Type of School

Aspirations	Type of School	
	Public School	Catholic School
No University	39	20
B.A.	39	60
Higher than B.A.	22	20
Total Per Cent	100	100
Number	18	104
Total N	122	
Missing Observations	5	

Chi-square = 3.53,
  d.f. = 2, n.s.
Cramer's V = 0.17

Hypothesis 8

> Among Croatian young people, the type of school one is presently attending does not have an effect on educational aspirations.

Table 8 indicates that there is no relationship between the type of school one attends and subjects' educational aspirations. Among those attending a public school, 39 per cent of the respondents aspire towards a university degree and 22 per cent aspire towards an education greater than a B.A. Among the respondents attending a Catholic school, 60 per cent aspire towards a university education and 20 per cent aspire towards an education greater than a B.A.

Table 8 shows that the type of school one attends is not significantly associated with one's educational aspirations; however, the limited association may be due to the disproportionate number of subjects attending Catholic high schools. The Chi-square for type of school was found to be 3.53 (df = 2, n.s.). The Cramer's V statistic was observed to be 0.17.

TABLE 9
Aspirations by Grades Received

Aspirations	Grades		
	Less than 60 per cent	70-79 per cent	80 per cent or above
No University	29	27	17
B.A.	53	60	55
Higher than B.A.	18	13	28
Total Per Cent	100	100	100
Number	17	52	53
Total N	122		
Missing Observations	5		

Chi-square = 4.55,
  d.f. = 4, n.s.
Gamma = 0.26

Thus, the data (Table 8) support the hypothesis that there is no association between the type of school one attends and one's educational aspirations. Therefore, the hypothesis may be accepted.

Hypothesis 9

> Among Croatian young people, the grades received in school do not have an effect on educational aspirations.

Table 9 shows that there is no relationship between received grades (marks) and educational aspirations. Of those students with grades in the category of less than 60 per cent, 53 per cent aspire towards university completion. Eighteen per cent of students in the same category wish to pursue education past their B.A.

Sixty per cent of students whose grades are in the 70 to 79 per cent category aspire towards completion of a B.A., while 13 per cent of students in the same category aspire towards an education higher than a B.A. Of those students whose grades are in the 80 per cent or greater category, 55

TABLE 10
Aspirations by Ability Compared with Close Friends

	Ability Compared with Close Friends		
Aspirations	Average or Below	Somewhat Above	Above Average
No University	32	28	8
B.A.	50	54	65
Higher than B.A.	18	18	27
Total Per Cent	100	100	100
Number	23	57	37
Total N	122		
Missing Observations	5		

Chi-square = 7.05,
 d.f. = 4, n.s.
Gamma = 0.29

per cent aspire towards university completion. Twenty-eight per cent of students in the same category wish to pursue their studies past a B.A.

Table 9 suggests that grades are not significantly associated with educational aspirations. The Chi-square for the grades received was found to be 4.55 (df = 4, n.s.). The gamma test of association was 0.26. Thus, the data (Table 9) support the hypothesis that there is no association between the grades one receives and one's educational aspirations. Therefore, the hypothesis may be accepted.

Hypothesis 10

> Among Croatian young people, one's perception of one's ability, as compared with close fiends, does not have an effect on educational aspirations.

Table 10 reveals that there is no relationship between how one perceives oneself in relation to one's friends' educational aspirations. Among those students who perceive themselves as "average or below," 50 per cent

TABLE 10A
Aspirations by Ability Compared with Close Friends

	Ability Compared with Close Friends		
Aspirations	Average or Below	Somewhat Above	Above Average
No University	32	28	8
University	68	72	92
Total Per Cent	100	100	100
Number	23	57	37
Total N	122		
Missing Observations	5		

Chi-square = 6.79,
  d.f. = 2, $p<0.05$
Gamma = 0.43

aspire towards a university education and 18 per cent wish to pursue an education beyond the B.A. level. Of those students who perceive themselves as "somewhat above average," 54 per cent aspire towards a university degree, and 18 per cent aspire to pursue their studies beyond a B.A. Finally, with reference to those respondents who perceive themselves as "above average" when compared with their close fiends, 65 per cent aspire towards a university degree and 27 per cent wish to continue their education beyond the B.A. level.

Table 10 reveals that the perception of one's ability as compared to one's close friends is not significantly associated with one's educational aspirations. The Chi-square for this analysis was found to be 7.05 (df = 4, n.s.). The gamma statistic of association was found to be 0.29, also suggesting no association between the two variables. Therefore, the data (Table 10) support the hypothesis that there is no association, thus it may be accepted.

Since there was a smaller number of respondents found in the higher than B.A. category, the following table (Table 10A) evaluates one's perception of one's ability as compared to one's close friends with only two categories of educational aspirations: "no university" and "university" aspirations.

Table 10A indicates that 68 per cent of those subjects who perceive themselves as "below average," 72 per cent of those who perceive themselves as "somewhat average," and 92 per cent of those who view themselves as "above average" aspire towards a university education.

This table confirms that there is a significant association between self-evaluation of ability and educational aspirations since the Chi-square was observed to be 6.79 (df = 2, p < .05). Similarly, the gamma measure of association reveals a tendency for the above-mentioned variables to be related, gamma = 0.43.

In comparing Table 10 to Table 10A we encounter a contradiction in the results. While ability influences the choice between university and no university streams, we suggest that ability does not have a significant effect on the level of aspirations within the university category.

Thus, the data (Table 10A) do not support the hypothesis of an association between one's perception of one's ability and educational aspirations. Therefore, it should be rejected.

Hypothesis 11

> Among Croatian young people, one's perception of one's ability, as compared with other classmates, does not have an effect on educational aspirations.

Table 11 shows that there is no relationship between how one perceives oneself in scholastic ability in relation to other classmates' educational aspirations. In reference to those respondents who perceive themselves as "average or below" when compared to other classmates, 57 per cent aspire towards a university degree and 13 per cent aspire towards an education beyond the B.A. level. Among those students who perceive themselves as "somewhat average" in relation to other classmates, 60 per cent aspire towards a university education and 17 per cent aspire towards an education beyond the B.A. level. Finally, 48 per cent of those students who view themselves as "above average" in relation to other classmates aspire towards a university degree and 37 per cent aspire towards an education greater than a B.A.

TABLE 11
Aspirations by Ability Compared with Classmates

Aspirations	Ability Compared with Classmates		
	Average or Below	Somewhat Above	Well Above Average
No University	30	23	15
B.A.	57	60	48
Higher than B.A.	13	17	37
Total Per Cent	100	100	100
Number	37	58	27
Total N	122		
Missing Observations	5		

Chi-square = 6.80, d.f. = 4, n.s.
Gamma = 0.29

Specifically, Table 11 confirms no association between one's self-evaluation of one's ability in comparison to one's classmates and educational aspirations, since the Chi-square was found to be 6.80 (df = 4, n.s.). Similarly, the gamma measure of association was also quite low at 0.29. Combined, these two measures confirm that there is no association between self-perception of scholastic ability with reference to classmates' educational aspirations. Thus, the above-mentioned hypothesis shows no association and may be accepted.

In order to get a clearer picture of the relationship between "aspirations" and "ability compared with classmates," Table 11A was dichotomized. As such, one's perception of one's ability as compared to classmates was examined with only two categories of educational aspirations: "no university," and "university" aspirations.

Table 11A indicates that 70 per cent of those subjects who perceived themselves as "average or below" aspired towards university completion. Seventy-seven per cent of subjects who felt that they were "somewhat above average" and 85 per cent who felt that they were "well above average" aspired towards a university education.

TABLE 11A
Aspirations by Ability Compared with Classmates

	Ability Compared with Classmates		
Aspirations	Average or Below	Somewhat Above	Well Above Average
No University	30	23	15
University	70	77	85
Total Per Cent	100	100	100
Number	37	58	27
Total N	122		
Missing Observations	5		
Chi-square = 1.98, d.f. = 2, n.s.			
Gamma = 0.25			

Once again Table 11A confirms no association between "aspirations" and "ability compared with classmates." In fact, the dichotomization of these variables resulted in a decrease in the value of the Chi-square (1.98, af = 2, n.s.), implying an even weaker association. The gamma measure of association was also observed to be lower (gamma = 0.25). Therefore, these measures confirm that there is no association between self-perception of scholastic ability and classmates' educational aspirations.

Hypothesis 12

> Among Croatian young people, one's perception of one's ability to graduate from university does not have an effect on educational aspirations.

Table 12 shows that there is a relationship between how one perceives one's ability to graduate from university and educational aspirations.

Referring to those respondents in the "not sure" category, 25 per cent aspire towards a university degree while 6 per cent aspire towards an education greater than a B.A. In the "probably" category, the numbers are

TABLE 12
Aspirations by Ability to Graduate from University

	Ability to Graduate from University		
Aspirations	Not Sure	Probably	Definitely
No University	69	22	10
B.A.	25	64	59
Higher than B.A.	6	14	31
Total Per Cent	100	100	100
Number	16	55	51
Total N	122		
Missing Observations	5		
Chi-square = 27.32, d.f. = 4, p<0.001			
Gamma = 0.57			

Not Sure: includes "not sure," "probably not," and "definitely not."

64 per cent aspiring towards a B.A. and 14 per cent aspiring higher than a B.A. Finally, in the "definitely" category, 59 per cent aspire towards a B.A. and 31 per cent aspire to greater than a B.A.

Consequently, Table 12 suggests that there is a relationship between the examined variables. The Chi-square amounts to 27.32 (df = 4, p<.001), and the gamma was found to be 0.57. Thus, the data in Table 12 do not support the hypothesis of the absence of an association between perception of one's ability to graduate from university and one's educational aspirations. Therefore, the hypothesis is rejected.

In order to further examine some of the inconsistencies of Table 12, such as some people desiring to do graduate work while not being sure they can get a B.A., or those subjects who are confident of their success but do not intend to try, we dichotomized the dependent variable into two categories: "no university" and "university" aspirations.

Table 12A illustrates the following results: 31 per cent of subjects are "not sure" they have the ability to graduate, 78 per cent "probably" feel they have the ability, and 90 per cent "definitely" feel they have the ability

TABLE 12A
Aspirations by Ability to Graduate from University

Aspirations	Ability to Graduate from University		
	Not Sure	Probably	Definitely
No University	69	22	10
University	31	78	90
Total Per Cent	100	100	100
Number	16	55	51
Total N	122		
Missing Observations	5		
Chi-square = 24.00, d.f. = 2, p<0.001			
Gamma = 0.67			

to graduate, all wish to attend university. Once again, Table 12A suggests that there is a strong relationship between the examined variables. The Chi-square was found to be 24.0 (df = 2, p<.001), and the gamma was observed to be 0.67. Thus, it has again been confirmed that there is a strong association between ability to graduate from university and educational aspirations. Therefore, the hypothesis should be rejected.

Hypothesis 13

> Among Croatian young poeple, one's perception of one's ability to complete a postgraduate degree does not have an effect on educational aspirations.

Table 13 shows a strong relationship between one's perception of ability to complete postgraduate work and educational aspirations. Referring to the "not sure" category, 43 per cent aspire towards a B.A., while 8 per cent would like to do postgraduate studies. Eighty per cent of those in the

TABLE 13
Aspirations by Ability to complete a Postgraduate Degree

	Ability to Complete a Postgraduate Degree		
Aspirations	Not Sure	Somewhat Likely	Very Likely
No University	49	10	11
B.A.	43	80	48
Higher than B.A.	8	10	41
Total Per Cent	100	100	100
Number	39	39	44
Total N	122		
Missing Observations	5		
Chi-square = 36.05,			
d.f. = 4, p<0.001			
Gamma = 0.61			

"somewhat likely" category would like to complete their B.A., while 10 per cent would like to continue past their B.A. In the "very likely" category, 48 per cent aspire towards a B.A. and 41 per cent aspire towards postgraduate education. As such, Table 13 suggests a strong relationship between perception of one's ability to complete postgraduate studies and one's educational aspirations; Chi-square = 36.05 (df = 4, $p < .001$), gamma = 0.61.

Hence, the data in Table 13 do not support the hypothesis of the absence of an association between perception of one's ability to do postgraduate studies and educational aspirations. Therefore, the hypothesis is rejected.

Hypothesis 14

> Among Croatian young people, one's country of birth does not have an effect on educational aspirations.

RESULTS

TABLE 14
Aspirations by Country of Birth

Aspirations	Country of Birth	
	Canada	Croatia
No University	21	33
B.A.	58	50
Higher than B.A.	21	17
Total Per Cent	100	100
Number	104	18
Total N	122	
Missing Observations	5	
Chi-square = 1.30,		
d.f. = 2, n.s.		
Cramer's V = 0.10		

Croatia: includes Croatia and countries other than Canada.

Table 14 reveals no relationship between one's country of birth and educational aspirations. With reference to those born in Canada, 58 per cent of the respondents aspire towards a university degree, while 21 per cent wish to continue their studies beyond the B.A. level. With reference to those born in Croatia, 50 per cent aspire towards a university degree, while 17 per cent wish to go beyond the B.A. level.

Subsequently, Table 14 suggests no association between one's country of origin and educational aspirations since the Chi-square was found to be 1.30 (df = 2, n.s.), and the Cramer's V statistic was observed to be 0.10. It should, however, be noted that there are very few observations in the "born in Croatia" category (18), which may have affected the level of significance.

As a result, the data in Table 14 support the hypothesis of no association between country of origin and educational aspirations. Thus, the hypothesis may be accepted.

TABLE 15
Aspirations by Place of Residence

Aspirations	Place of Residence	
	City	Other
No University	21	36
B.A.	57	57
Higher than B.A.	22	7
Total Per Cent	100	100
Number	106	14
Total N	120	
Missing Observations	7	
Chi-square = 2.35,		
d.f. 2, n.s.		
Cramer's V = 0.14		

Other: includes small town, village, and other.

Hypothesis 15

> Among Croatian young people, one's place of residence does not have an effect on educational aspirations.

Table 15 shows no relationship between place of residence and educational aspirations. Looking at the "city" category, we can see that 57 per cent of respondents aspire towards a B.A., while 22 per cent aspire towards education higher than a B.A. Fifty-seven per cent of respondents fitting the "other" category aspire towards a B.A. and 7 per cent aspire towards postgraduate education.

Thus, Table 15 shows no association between place of residence and educational aspirations. The Chi-square amounted to 2.35 (df = 2, n.s.), and Cramer's V was observed to be 0.14. However, these results may have been affected by the small number of observations in the "other" category.

As a result, the data in Table 15 support the hypothesis of no association between place of residence and educational aspirations. Thus, the hypothesis may be accepted.

RESULTS

TABLE 16
Aspirations by Number of Siblings

Aspirations	Number of Siblings			
	One	Two	Three	Four
No University	25	23	26	17
University	75	77	74	83
Total Per Cent	100	100	100	100
Number	4	44	434	29
Total N	120			
Missing Observations	7			

Chi-square = 0.71,
  d.f. = 3, n.s.
Gamma = 0.08

Hypothesis 16

> Among Croatian young people, the number of siblings in the family does not have an effect on educational aspirations.

Table 16 shows no relationship between number of siblings and educational aspirations. Of those subjects who reflect the "only child" category, 75 per cent aspire towards a university education. Seventy-seven per cent of subjects in the "two children" category, 74 per cent in the "three children" category, and 83 per cent in the "four or more children" category aspire towards a university education.

The results (Table 16) show no association between the number of siblings and educational aspirations. The Chi-square equalled 0.71 (df = 3, n.s.), and the gamma was found to be 0.08.

Consequently, the data in Table 16 support the hypothesis of no association between number of siblings and educational aspirations. Thus, the hypothesis may be accepted.

TABLE 17
Aspirations by Birth Order

Aspirations	Birth Order		
	First Born	Second Born	Third Born or Higher
No University	18	22	42
B.A.	61	61	32
Higher than B.A.	21	17	26
Total Per Cent	100	100	100
Number	57	46	19
Total N	122		
Missing Observations	5		

Chi-square = 6.82, d.f. = 4, n.s.
Gamma = -0.15

Hypothesis 17

> Among Croatian young people, birth order does not have an effect on educational aspirations.

Table 17 shows no relationship between birth order and educational aspirations. Sixty-one per cent of "first born" subjects aspire towards a B.A., while 21 per cent of the subjects in the same category aspire towards education higher than a B.A. Sixty-one per cent of "second born" subjects aspire towards a B.A., while 17 per cent in the same category aspire towards education higher than a B.A. In the "third born or higher" category, the respective percentages were 32 per cent and 26 per cent.

The results in Table 17 show no association between birth order and educational aspirations. The Chi-square was found to be 6.892 (df = 4, n.s.), and the gamma = -0.15.

RESULTS

TABLE 17A
Aspirations by Birth Order

Aspirations	Birth Order		
	First Born	Second Born	Third Born or Higher
No University	18	22	42
University	82	78	58
Total Per Cent	100	100	100
Number	57	46	19
Total N	122		
Missing Observations	5		

Chi-square = 4.92,
   d.f. = 2, p<0.10
Gamma -0.32

As such, data in Table 17 support the hypothesis of no association between birth order and educational aspirations. Thus, the hypothesis may be accepted.

In order to examine possible differences between birth order and educational aspirations, the variable aspirations was dichotomized into no university and university.

It was found that 82 per cent of first borns, 78 per cent of second borns, and 58 per cent of third borns or higher wished to complete a university education. Thus results in Table 17A show no association between birth order and educational aspirations. The Chi-square was found to be 4.92 (df = 2, p<.10). The gamma measure of association was found to be -0.32. Thus, in dichotomizing educational aspirations, it was found that the Chi-square approaches significance, implying some association between birth order and educational aspirations. Therefore, the hypothesis should be rejected.

MULTIPLE REGRESSION ANALYSIS

In order to arrive at a deeper understanding of the relationship between our variables, multiple regression analysis was used.

The purpose of the first task is to predict the values of the dependent variable, educational aspirations, on the basis of the values of several independent variables, which the review of the literature has suggested are very strong predictors. Particluarly, we were interested in the relationship of the independent variables concerned with socio-economic origin, such as father's education, mother's education, father's occupation, mother's occupation, and family income.

The betas, also known as the standardized regression coefficients, are low, implying a very weak relationship between the independent variables and the dependent variable. Table 18 lists the betas for the independent variables: income, mother's occupation. It is important to note that most of the beta coefficients are negative. These findings directly contradict the results observed by other researchers who have examined these traditional predictors and found most to be positive.

Table 18 also reports the R-square to be .097 and the Adjusted R-square to be .034. This simply refers to the fact that only 3.4 per cent of the variance in educational aspirations is explained by the above-mentioned socio-economic status variables.

Thus, the data in Table 18 show that the independent variables, income, mother's occupation, father's occupation, father's education, and mother's education, are not good predictors of the dependent variable, educational aspirations. This supports the hypothesis that there is no association between subjects' aspirations and the above-mentioned independent variables.

In order to eliminate other sources of influence, a larger multiple regression model was analyzed. Once again, this model explored the relationship between several independent variables, including the socio-economic origin variables, as well as other variables that this study found to have some predictive value, and the dependent variable, educational aspirations.

Specifically, we predicted the values of the dependent variable, educational aspirations, on the basis of the values of several independent

TABLE 18
Multiple Regression of Aspirations by Family Income, Mother's Occupation, Father's Occupation, Father's Occupation, and Mother's Education

Independent Variable	Betas
Income	-0.098
Mother's Occupation	0.050
Father's Occupation	-0.007
Father's Education	-0.153
Mother's Occupation	-0.329
R-square = 0.097	
Adjusted R-square = 0.034	

Educational Aspirations

variables, such as gender, ability compared with close friends, ability compared with classmates, ability to graduate from university, and ability to complete a postgraduate degree. Included in this model were the previously examined socio-economic origin variables.

Table 19 reports the R-square to be 0.292. The Adjjusted R-square was found to be 0.184. These figures suggest that 18.4 per cent of the variance in educational aspirations is explained by the above-mentioned independent variables. Upon examination of the betas, we once again found that overall they were low and negative.

Table 20 explores this relationship further. In this table we eliminated the socio-economic origin variables and examined only the influence of such variables as gender, ability to graduate from university, and ability to complete a postgraduate degree. The R-square was found to be 0.264, which suggests that 23.2 per cent of the variance in educational aspirations is explained by these variables.

The data in tables 18 through 20 suggest that the socio-economic origin variables have limited predictive value. The elimination of these variables in Table 20 increases the Adj. R-square, thus further supporting our hypothesis that the socio-economic variables are not good predictors of

TABLE 19
Multiple Regression of Aspirations by Income, Mother's Education, Father's Occupation, Father's Education, Mother's Occupation, Gender, Ability Compared with Close Friends, Ability Compared with Classmates, Ability to Graduate from University, and Ability to Complete Postgraduate Degree

Educational Aspirations

Independent Variable	Betas
Income	-0.092
Mother's Education	0.011
Father's Occupation	-0.007
Father's Education	-0.036
Mother's Occupation	-0.189
Gender	0.144
Ability Compared with Close Friends	-0.066
Ability Compared with Classmates	0.164
Ability to Graduate from University	-0.309
Ability to Complete Postgraduate Degree	-0.238
R-square = 0.292	
Adjusted R-square = 0.184	

the dependent variable, educational aspirations. Hence, Croatian youths have high aspirations simply because they are highly motivated to achieve success for themselves.

SUMMARY

The hypotheses that have been tested have given us ample opportunity to investigate the various predictors affecting educational aspiration formation among Croatian high school students. Our findings will be elaborated upon in the following chapter.

RESULTS

TABLE 20

Multiple Regression of Aspirations by Gender, Ability Compared with Close Friends, Ability Compared with Classmates, Ability to Graduate from University, and Ability to Complete Postgraduate University

Independent Variable	Educational Aspirations Betas
Gender	0.149
Ability Compared with Close Friends	-0.070
Ability Compared with Classmates	0.159
Ability to Graduate from University	-0.330
Ability to Complete Postgraduate Degree	-0.258
R-square = 0.264	
Adjusted R-square = 0.232	

CHAPTER SIX

Discussion

After analyzing our data, we have finally arrived at the task of explaining how our original hypothesis fared. We proposed that Croatian youth, despite their background limitations, will have fairly high aspirations. Indeed, as our results have shown 87 per cent of the subjects aspired towards some form of post-secondary education. At a closer examination, the figures pointed out that 77 per cent of subjects aspired towards a university education.

SOCIO-ECONOMIC ORIGIN VARIABLES

It is well to begin with the variables that we found produced the most compelling results. In the literature, family income, father's education, mother's occupation, mother's education, and father's occupation are identified as socio-economic origin variables.

Research on the relationship of these variables continually shows that they are strong predictors of educational aspirations. In studying the aspirations of Anglo-Canadian, West Indian, and South European high school students in Ontario, Calliste concluded that students who came from lower socio-economic backgrounds are likely to have lower educational aspirations than students from higher socio-economic backgrounds. In her sample of 892 subjects, she stated that four out of ten students of lower socio-economic background expected to go to university or college (Calliste, 1980:203).

Breton (1970) studied educational and occupational expectations of 144,960 students attending 373 randomly selected Canadian high schools in 1965. While his study assessed the impact of a number of sociological and psychological variables, we will focus on the reported effects of socio-economic background.

Breton used father's education and father's occupation as socio-economic variables. As such, these socio-economic status variables revealed a great deal of influence on post-secondary expectations. It was reported that 86.1 per cent of males and 82.7 per cent of females whose parents were in the highest social class (managerial and professional) aspired towards post-secondary education. For those students whose fathers were in the lowest category (unskilled and farming) the comparative figures were 69.3 per cent and 70.6 per cent, respectively (Breton, 1970:25).

The findings of the present study showed no relationship between the socio-economic origin variables and the distribution of educational aspirations. In other words, students from lower socio-economic backgrounds have aspirations similar to students in higher socio-economic backgrounds. This unique finding may be the result of the limited number of middle-class Croatians in our sample. As such, the small number of middle-class Croatians in our sample has the same level of aspirations as working-class Croatians. In this respect, they do not yet reflect the traditional socio-economically related, class distinct, educational achievement patterns of North American youth.

In order to arrive at a better understanding of the relationship between the socio-economic origin variables and their influence on educational aspirations, regression analysis was used. We found that the variables father's education, mother's occupation, father's occupation, mother's education, and family income only accounted for 3.4 per cent of the variance in the dependent variable educational aspirations. We also noted that the beta coefficients for the above-mentioned variables, with the exception of mother's education (beta = .05), are negative. Both observations suggest that the traditional predictors of post-secondary aspirations do not hold much value for Croatian youths.

Thus, the present study does not confirm the literature's consistent findings of the impact of socio-econmic background on educational

DISCUSSION

aspirations. For instance, Porter, Porter, and Blishen (1982) studied the post-secondary aspirations of 9000 students attending 400 junior and high schools in Ontario in 1971. They appraised the effects of parental education on students' aspirations. The authors noted that 25 per cent of students whose parents had low levels of education wanted to go to university. The comparative figure for students whose parents had high levels of education was 63 per cent (Porter et al., 1982:91). The authors further reported that 59 per cent of females and 66 per cent of males belonging to the top social class (physicians, lawyers, engineers) wanted to graduate from university. Of those students belonging to the lowest class (unskilled, truck drivers, janitors), 22 per cent of females and 35 per cent of males wanted to graduate from university (ibid., 1982:59). Within their study, it is evident that students' aspirations are aligned with parental social status and, as such, the students' social and educational class position may be inherited from their parents.

For the Croatian sample, social status difference did not matter. Croatian students did not see their parents' status as an obstacle to their own aspirations. When family income was cross-tabulated with aspirations, our results showed that 92 per cent of subjects whose family income was less than $35,000 per year wanted to, at the very least, complete university. The comparable figure for those whose family income was over $60,000 was 81 per cent.

Interestingly, only 62 per cent of the subjects whose family income was in the $35,001 to $60,000 category wanted to, at the very least, complete university education. Thus, one may argue that middle-class Croatian youth are being held back. However, within this Croatian sample, the traditional North American socio-economically related linear pattern of educational aspiration is not reflected.

Further regression analyses were utilized in order to arrive at a better understanding of the association between socio-economic origin variables and their relationship to educational aspiration formation among Croatian youth. We found that when we added variables, which were previously observed to be strongly related to educational aspiration formation, the predictive value of the model increased (from 3 to 18 per cent). From our cross-tabular analyses, these variables included: gender, ability compared with close friends, ability compared with classmates, ability to graduate from university, and ability to complete a postgraduate degree.

However, by removing the socio-economic origin variables from the model and studying the association between the independent variables:

gender, ability compared with close friends, ability compared with Classmates, ability to graduate from university, and ability to complete postgraduate degree, and the dependent variable educational aspirations, we observed that the predictive power of the model increased. Thus, these consequent analyses further strengthen our argument. Accordingly, regardless of their own socio-economic status, Croatian parents instilled the importance of a university education in their children.

A question measuring the extent of parental encouragement of the subjects' post-secondary education was phrased in the following fashion: "In general, to what extent have each of the following people encouraged or discouraged you to continue your education after high school: mother or father?" On a five-point scale "discouraged you very much" was the lowest category (number 1) and "encouraged you very much" was the highest category (number 5). Within the highest category (category 5), subjects reported that 73 per cent of fathers and 71 per cent of mothers encouraged them to pursue post-secondary education.

At this time, we should illustrate how our parental sample compared to the Canadian population. Based on data from the 1981 census, we compared our sample to both Canadian and Croatian categories. On average, our subjects' parents completed just under 11 years of formal education. This figure is slightly under the Canadian average of 11.56 years, and the Croatian average of 11.12 years. The Croatian category within the census included Croatians, Serbians, Slovenes, and Yugoslavs. Seventy-three per cent of the subjects' parents worked in unskilled or skilled jobs. The comparable figure for the Croatian category in the census is 77 per cent. Census figures show that the average "workers" category is 70 per cent. Thus, our sample was slightly lower than the Croatian unskilled and skilled categories in the census and slightly higher than the Canadian unskilled and skilled categories (1981 Census of Canada, Public Use Sample Tape, Cat 92911).

We can tentatively suggest that our sample reflected the general composition of the Croatian population living in Canada. While their family income was higher than the Canadian average, they tended to be overrepresented in semi-skilled manufacturing. Concurrently, their level of education tended to be lower than the Canadian average.

In a study of ethnic inequality in Canada, Li (1988) addressed the question of whether ethnicity has an impact on educational and economic success. Utilizing previously unpublished data from the 1981 census, he compared economic and educational success rates for 17 ethnic and racial

DISCUSSION

groups, including Jewish, British, French, German, Dutch, Scandinavian, Greek, Italian, Portuguese, Croatian, Czech and Slovak, Hungarian, Polish, Ukranian, Black, Chinese, and Other. Of interest to our study were his findings of Croatians. In particular, Li studied the net effects of ethnicity on educational attainment. Using a multivariate regression analysis model of one dependent variable (level of schooling) and four independent variables (ethnic origin, gender, nativity, age) he looked at the net effects of ethnic origin on educational attainment.

Those ethnic groups whose scores fell below the mean had a net origin associated disadvantage. This disadvantage was present regardless of the effects of age, income, nativity, or gender. Ethnic groups who scored above the mean had a net advantage associated with their origin.

Adjusting for differences in nativity and gender, Li found that Croatians had a -0.60 level of schooling below the Canadian average. After adjusting for variations in age, gender, and nativity, Croatians had -0.76 years of schooling less than the average Canadian.

Croatians' standings among other East European groups (Czech and Slovak: 1.02; Hungarian: 0.33; Ukranian: 0.06; Polish: -0.02) was the lowest. Indeed, among the 17 ethno-racial groups that were compared, Croatians were fourth from the bottom, the lowest being Portuguese (-4.14), Italians (-2.19), and Greeks (-1.95). The group that benefited the most from their ethnic origin were the Jews with 1.80 years of schooling more than the average Canadian's 11.56 years of schooling (Li, 1988:109-113).

Looking at university attendance, we can see that, according to the 1981 census, 10.28 per cent of all Canadians completed a university education. Croatians, with 9.36 per cent, placed eleventh among the seventeen groups (ibid., 1988:76). Croats who completed university within our sample showed the following results: 3.2 per cent of our subjects' mothers and 5.5 per cent of their fathers completed university. This figure is both below the Canadian average and the Croatian average on the 1981 census.

If we compare our sample with other ethnic groups, we can observe that only the Portuguese (1.3) and the Greeks (5.43) had lower university attainment rates. On the other side of the spectrum, 32.06 per cent of Jews, and 20.67 per cent of Chinese had completed a university education (Li, 1988:76).

As the literature has pointed out, many factors account for uneven university access. Among these, ethnic origin is of importance, particularly in the way it shapes educators' perceptions of students.

Along this line of thought, the present study wanted to examine how our subjects perceived themselves in comparison to traditionally high university attainment groups (Jewish, Chinese) and low attainment groups (Portuguese, Italian).

The question addressing this issue was phrased in the following fashion:

> Do you believe that you, as a Croat or of Croatian background, have the same, better, or worse chance than someone of Jewish background; Chinese, or someone of Chinese background; Portuguese, or someone of Portuguese background; Italian, or someone of Italian background...to get accepted into university?

Forty-seven per cent of our subjects felt that they had the same chance, and 45 per cent felt that they had a worse chance than omeone of Jewish background of getting accepted into university. Comparable figures for someone of Chinese background were 76 per cent and 15 per cent.

Comparing our subjects with their perceptions of someone of Italian background, it was found that 87 per cent felt that they had the same chance and 2 per cent felt that they had a worse chance of getting into university.

Comparable figures for someone of Portuguese background, were 81 per cent and 1 per cent, respectively.

Thus, our subjects did not perceive that their ethnic origin was detrimental to university access. In general, the majority did not feel that any other ethnic or racial group had a better chance of gaining university access.

Concurrently, Croatian youths have extremely high aspirations regardless of their socio-economic origin. This may be the result of a number of factors. In particular, their parents have inculcated into them the ideal that education is extremely important for success. It could also be reflective of the fact that Croatians, from a family income point of view, have fared better than the average Canadian.

Still, according to the Croatian category within the 1981 census, 76.7 per cent are represented as workers (employees in occupations that do not allow for much autonomy over their work and not much control over their own labour); 10.1 per cent are represented as professionals; 4.3 per cent as managers; and 4.3 per cent as self-employed without paid help (Li, 1988:68-71; 88-94).

DISCUSSION

Within our sample, Croatians felt that in order to gain social status they needed further education. However, money alone was not a good indicator of status. As such, they felt that in order to gain recognition and social status they needed further education. They have shown that financially they have fared much better than their counterparts in Croatia and are quite competitive in the Canadian market. However, they still want to do better, and one way of doing this is through the success of their children. Since in most instances they themselves could not attend university, it is important for their children to do so. In this fashion, they have projected their own sense of success onto their children. Almost every Croatian parent encountered in the preparation of this study exclaimed how proud they would be if their child became a physician, dentist, or lawyer.

DEMOGRAPHIC VARIABLES

In discussing demographic variables, we will consider gender, number of siblings, birth order, country of birth, and place of residence.

So that we may be able to generalize our results, we have compared our findings with two of the most comprehensive Canadian studies in the area of educational aspirations. Calliste (1980) and Porter, Porter, and Blishen (1982) undertook extensive research on the influence of demographic variables on aspiration formation.

In our study, academic success for both males and females was of great importance. Specifically, 70 per cent of males and 82 per cent of females aspired towards university completion.

Commenting on the differences of aspirations between the sexes, Porter, Porter, and Blishen (1982) suggested that in the early stages of high school, females are more successful in terms of grade achievement. However, in later grades their success tapers off. During this stage, it is the males who are more successful: "for boys, education becomes intrinsically linked to future occupations...in the minds of girls...education is less important to future identity and success..." (ibid., 1982:213).

Calliste (1980) studied the relationship between gender and aspirations among a sample of Anglo-Canadians (students of Irish, Scottish, and English ancestry), Europeans (students of Greek or Italian origin), and West Indians (students of West Indian origin). She reported that of her total sample, 40 per cent of females and 52 per cent of males expected post-secondary education.

The female student population of our sample came out with much higher aspirations. Specifically, when we compared our results with Calliste's (1980), we observed that twice as many Croatian females aspired to graduate from university. Again, it should be noted that our sample was skewed in favour of females.

Recent statistics illustrate that in Canada, since 1981, there has been a significant increase in the number of female graduates. For instance, in 1981, 6.5 per cent of Canadian females 15 years of age and older had a university degree. In 1985, 8.3 per cent were university graduates in Canada. Therefore, in just five years, the figure increased by almost two per cent (Education in Canada: A Statistical Review 1986:259).

Hence, it can be argued that the females in our sample reflect the changing trends in the role of women and educational attainment. They do not reflect Porter, Porter, and Blishen's perception that women "loath to plan for occupations...because they consider their future roles as wives and mothers to be primary goals and anything else to be, if necessary, basically undesirable" (1982:213).

The social climate in Canada, in general, and Ontario, in particular, reflects the opinion that women are expected to work during motherhood. In view of the economic strains on today's young families, it is often expected that the woman will have to balance her roles as wife, mother, and provider. A review of 18 to 21 year olds enrolled in a Canadian university undergraduate programme, related to the same age cohort of the general population, provided the following illustration. In 1981, 11.3 per cent of age related females attended university. In 1985-86, the figure represented 13.4 per cent, an increase of over 2 per cent. Comparable figures for the males were 11.2 and 12.5 per cent, respectively, an increase of 1.3 per cent. (Education in Canada: A Statistical Review, 1986:134).

Looking at the figures for Ontario, the following results were observed. In 1981, 21.2 per cent of the 18- to 21-year-old female age group attended university. In 1985-86, 26.1 per cent of females attended university. This represents an increase of almost 5 per cent. The figures for the males were 24.1 and 26.0 per cent, respectively, an increase of just under 2 per cent. Almost one-half of university undergraduates were women (ibid., 1986:52).

Thus, in optimizing their occupational potential, the females in our sample reflected the thinking that education for them was more important then it was for the boys.

DISCUSSION

Variables such as number of siblings and birth order offered us the following results. While the results were non-significant, we found that those subjects who had families with four or more siblings had higher aspirations than those with two or less siblings. Opposite results were found by Porter, Porter, and Blishen (1982) who showed that the highest percentage of students wishing to attend university were those whose families included one or two children. This was regardless of the family's socio-economic status.

As far as birth order is concerned, we found that 82 per cent of first borns wanted to attend university. Of the second borns, 78 per cent wished to attend university, and finally, of the third borns, 58 per cent wanted to attend university. If we relate the number of siblings to birth order, we may observe that those coming from the largest families are most likely to aspire to university, yet the younger children in large families are the least likely to aspire towards university completion. This may be due to the fact that most of our subjects belonged to large (three or more children) families.

In view of the rising costs of education, we are concerned that regardless of socio-economic background, large families will find it more difficult to keep their children in university.

The two remaining demographic variables are country of birth and place of residence. Our study showed that those students born in Canada had slightly higher aspirations than those born in Croatia. These figures should be viewed with some discrimination since most of our sample reflected the fact that 85 per cent of our subjects were born in Canada. Of the remaining 15 per cent, all came to Canada under the age of 10 years.

Place of residence is another demographic variable that we viewed. We found that 79 per cent of subjects born in the city and 64 per cent of subjects born in a small town or village wanted to attend university. These figures show that urban subjects had higher aspirations, although the difference is not significant.

Similar findings were reported by Porter, Porter, and Blishen (1982). While they suggested that educational aspirations are related to the degree of urbanization, our results should be viewed discriminantly, since 86 per cent of our subjects live in the Toronto corridor.

SCHOOL VARIABLES

In discussing school variables, we will consider grade level of student, type of school attended (Catholic or public), and grades received (student reported).

When we examined the grade level variable, we found that as students progressed through high school their aspirations towards university completion diminished. For instance, of those students attending grade 10, 84 per cent wanted to complete university. Of our subjects who were attending grade 12, 58 per cent wanted to do the same. This type of finding is to be expected since, as students progress through high school, their views of educational opportunity become more realistic. They may feel that while they want to attend university, they are not able to for reasons over which they have no control. As such, their aspirations may fall in line with opting out for something that is at least financially rewarding.

When we looked at the student reported grade variable, we found a linear progression. Seventy-one per cent of subjects who had less than 60 per cent average wanted to go to university. The figure for those students receiving grades between 70 to 79 per cent was 73 per cent. Comparable figures for those with an average of 80 per cent or better was 83 per cent. It should be noted that 86 per cent of our sample received grades higher than a B or 70 per cent.

Similar results were found by Calliste (1982). When she broke down the category by ethnic background, she reported that 35 per cent of Anglo-Canadians who reported grades of B or better aspired towards post-secondary education. Her results for South Europeans (Greeks and Italians) showed a 10 per cent increase (45 per cent). Thus, comparing our Croatian subjects with Calliste's Anglo-Canadian sample shows that for every one of her Anglo-Canadian subjects who wished to attend a post-secondary institution, there were almost three Croatians with similar aspirations. Comparing our subjects to her South European samples we can see that the ratio of Croatians to that of Calliste's South European sample wanting to attend post-secondary education is two to one. This may be the result of the fact that Calliste's South European sample consisted of traditionally low educational attainment groups.

Finally we looked at the type of school. We wanted to see if there was a difference in the aspirations of students attending Catholic versus public high schools. While we found that the students attending Catholic high schools had higher aspirations than those attending public high schools, the difference was too small to be significant.

SELF-CONCEPT OF ABILITY

The following variables were considered when analyzing the self-concept of ability variable: rating yourself in school ability with close friends, rating yourself in school ability with your classmates, and having the academic ability to graduate from university.

When we observed the variable, rating yourself in school ability with your close friends, we found some linearity. Particularly, those subjects who felt that their ability was above average had the highest aspirations. Ninety-two per cent of the subjects in that group wanted to, at the very least, graduate from university. Of those subjects who were in the average or below category in ability, 68 per cent wanted to graduate from a university. While our findings reflect those by Porter et al. (1982), they are not as extreme. They reported that 65 per cent of their grade 10 cohort who had a high self-concept of ability wanted to go to university, while only six per cent of those with a low self-concept of ability wanted to do the same (1982:88). Thus, the difference in the two categories amounts to 59 per cent. Among the Croatian sample, the difference was 24 per cent.

When we looked at the variable, ability compared with classmates, we found similar results. Of those whose ability was above average, 85 per cent wanted to attend university, while 70 per cent whose ability was average or below average wanted to do the same. This time, however, the results were non-significant.

When we looked at the variable, ability to graduate from university, we once again found some linearity. Ninety per cent of our subjects felt that they definitely had the ability to graduate from university. Seventy-eight per cent believed that they would probably graduate, while 30 per cent were not sure.

In comparing our results to Calliste's (1980) findings, we looked at the highest category; that is, we wanted to see how our subjects in the definite category compared. Thirty-six per cent of Anglo-Canadians, 45 per cent of West Indians, and 46 per cent of South Europeans felt that they had a definite ability to graduate from university (1980:113). Ninety per cent of our Croatian subjects who definitely have the ability aspired to graduate from university. Thus, within this category, for every one Anglo-Canadian there were three Croatians who aspired to graduate. Similarly, a comparison of Croatians to West Indians and South Europeans produced a two to one ratio.

Self-concept of ability among our Croatian sample seems to be quite high. Our subjects reflect the literature findings, which suggest that those students who have a great deal of academic confidence have high aspirations. For example, studies by Reitzes and Mutran (1980), Anisef (1973), and Maxwell and Maxwell (1984) all concur that self-concept of ability is very important in delineating educational aspirations among high school youths.

SUMMARY

In this chapter we have explained how our hypotheses fared.

Our most compelling finding suggests that, among Croatian youths, socio-economic origin variables do not have a strong influence in educational aspiration-formation processes.

The next and final chapter will deal with and conclude upon these issues.

CHAPTER SEVEN

Conclusions

This research successfully examined the effects of a number of variables the literature found to be important in the formation of educational aspirations, and their relationship to Croatian high school students. Specifically, we examined the effects such independent variables as: socio-economic origin, gender, ethnic origin, regional origin, religious origin, peer influence, parental influence, self-concept, and perception of opportunity had on the formation of educational aspirations among Croatian high school students in Toronto and vicinity.

Despite their background limitations, we found that Croatian high school students have extremely high aspirations. Most compellingly, we observed that for Croatian youth socio-economic origin variables were not characteristically influential in their decisions to pursue a university education.

LIMITATIONS OF THE STUDY

The major limitation of the present study was that a small sample of 127 subjects was used. This number may not appear small at first glance, however, when compared to Calliste's (1980) 892 subjects, and Porter, Porter, and Blishen's (1982) sample, which consisted of 9000 students, the present sample seems quite small. One should note that larger samples are more likely to result in statistical significances. Thus, the present study was somewhat limited since it contained fewer subjects and as a result, a lesser chance of finding significant relationships between educational aspirations and school, socio-economic, demographic, and self-concept of ability variables. However, the author feels that since only one ethnic group was studied, the sample size of 127 is more than sufficient to analyze the educational aspirations of young Croatians in Toronto.

Another related limitation stemmed from the selection of the sample. The present study did not employ a random sampling technique, but rather used a purposive sampling procedure. This method allowed the researcher the opportunity to develop an increasing set of observations through the recommendation of other subjects by present participants. Although such a procedure may have limited the present study, the author feels that it was the only applicable one in this specific study since one cannot obtain information on ethnicity through the school boards. Hence, if one wishes to study any ethnic group, specifically Croatians, one needs to employ a non-random selection procedure.

Another shortcoming of the present study was the higher proportion of females to males in the sample. This would simply result in more accurate findings for females than for males. The final limitation concerned the researcher's collapsing of the variables in the cross-tabular analysis of educational aspirations on the school, socio-economic, demographic, and self-concept of ability variables. The author felt that it was most frequently useful to dichotomize educational aspirations into two categories: university and no university. As well, a number of independent variables were collapsed into two or more categories. These procedures may have resulted in a loss of information. However, the author attempted to and succeeded in maintaining this loss at a minimum.

The limitations of the present study should be corrected in future research by attempting to consider a larger and perhaps more representative probability sample of the entire Croatian population living in Canada. Similarly, future researchers should employ a sampling technique whereby a more equalized proportion of the sexes exists. In order to achieve a greater balance in future research, qualitative techniques should also be applied. This would, for the researcher as well as the reader, offer greater insight into the problem.

CONCLUSION

A major conclusion in this study is that socio-economic origin variables do not have a significant impact on educational aspiration formation among Croatian adolescents. This finding is incongruent to a number of Canadian studies (Calliste, 1980; Porter, Porter, and Blishen, 1982; Anisef et al., 1986) that suggest the importance of socio-econoimc origin variables in the formation of a student's educational aspirations.

Furthermore, we suggest that ethnic background could be an important precursor to the optimization of educational and consequently occupational potential. Thus, we agree with Li (1988) that ethnic origin has a definite educational and occupational market value. For some ethnic groups, like Jews, ethnic origin is extremely advantageous, both educationally and occupationally, while for Portuguese it is extremely disadvantageous (Li, 1988:135-137). Li concludes that ethnic origin has an absolute impact on educational and occupational disparities:

> the results of these disparities is that ethnic groups are distinguishable on the basis of their relative position in the income structure of Canada. To this extent; it is correct to say that ethnic groups are stratified in Canada.... With respect to the question of whether there is equal opportunity for all ethnic origins, our evidence clearly suggests that ethnicity provides a net advantage for some groups and a net disadvantage for others (Li, 1988:140).

If, as Li suggests, this is the case, we can take the position that the educational institutions could play a very important role in eradicating these differences. Our Croatian subjects, regardless of their socio-economic background, showed a strong inclination towards university completion. If optimization of their goals is hindered by events over which they have no control, we can suggest that Croats may be stereotyped as early school leavers, and thus streamed into non-universtiy educational tracks.

Consequently, when we looked at a number of psycho-demographic variables, we once again found that, on the whole, Croatian adolescents were attracted to university education in overwhelming numbers.

It is interesting that the census portrays this group as financially successful. Li (1988) suggested that for Croatians ethnic origin is economically advantageous, yet educationally it is disadvantageous.

We strongly believe that for Croatians, culture and ethnic identity influenced this as well as the major findings of the present study. We propose that the high level of aspirations Croatians hold relate to particular features of their culture and their experiences before or since coming to Canada. Like the traditionally high achieving groups, their ambition may be related to their historical experiences.

In former Yugoslavia, Croats were a minority, in some instances (Croatian Spring, 1971) struggling for greater autonomy of language, culture, and identity. While going through their own process of ethnogenesis, Croats, for the first time in modern history, can claim a piece of land they call their own. The Republic of Croatia was proclaimed on 15 January 1992. Croats in Canada are a tightly knit homogeneous group whose goals are to uphold their language, culture, and identity. While it is important to integrate into the mainstream Canadian lifestyle, it is also important to remain faithful to the Croatian ideal of helping members achieve optimum success.

As a measure of success their primary goal was to succeed financially. Once this was achieved, most often through unskilled, semi-skilled, or skilled jobs they felt that their next task was to instil this ethic in their children. However, it was important that their children achieve success through education, for in their eyes education is not only a sign of prestige, but also a way into a career that does not require manual forms of labour. It is also a commonly held belief among Croatians that education is portable and transferable, since historically they were labelled a highly transitory group.

Having commented on the historical implications, our final task is to focus attention on the role of the educational system and any pertinent policy implications.

If ethnic children, in general, and Croatians, in particular, show an interest in post-secondary education, then the educational decision-makers (teachers, guidance couisellors) should be sensitive to ethnic-cultural differences and work towards optimizing every child's educational potential. The role of the teachers should be to motivate all students to optimize this potential. They should recognize the diversity of ethnic backgrounds rather than digress from them and should move beyond the basic multicultural school trends such as ethnic dancing, food, and music.

An article dealing with minorities and education comments that "the most prevalent form of discrimination is a kind of paternalism...that allows you not to respect, that allows you not to demand...often what wwe expect a student to do becomes what they can do" (*Toronto Star*, April 21, 1989:A6).

In order to avoid potential discrimination, those children whose parents are unfamiliar with the Canadian educational system, in general, and Ontario's, in particular, lack the appropriate communication skills, should be sensitized to a number of educational options available to them. They should be exposed to views that would allow them unbiased access to post-secondary education if they so desire. University access, while relying on a minimum grade entrance requirement, should guarantee access to all those who have achieved it.

Nevertheless, a recent study of 5000 first year students attending six Canadian universities including the University of Western Ontario, University of Guelph, Lakehead University, University of Windsor, Simon Fraser University, and Laurentian University found that the students came from well off, stable (only 15 per cent of the students came from divorced families at a time when Canadian divorce rates were estimated at 40 per cent) middle-class families. Twenty-five per cent of students within one of the above universities reported a family income greater than $100,000. Only five per cent reported a family income of $20,000 or less. The median family income in Ontario, at the completion of the study was $40,500 (*The Toronto Star*, March 18, 1989:D1).

Our own government is seemingly lame in trying to alleviate such discrepancies. The federal government in 1977 stopped sharing the financial costs of post-secondary education with the provinces. While the government substituted some tax room to the provinces, this was not nearly enough to offset the unprecedently large number of new post-secondary students. Canadians today spend $440.00 per capita on research and post-secondary education (Cameron, 1981), a figure that in our eyes is extremely low considering Canada's position in the developed world. As Cameron (1987) points out: "Per-student university grants...fell by 30 per cent in constant dollars between 1974-75 and 1983-84, using the Consumer Price Index as the measure of inflation" (1987:11).

As such, universities may have to further curtail access and, as a result, a number of our children who have the aspirations and the necessary minimum requirements will not be in a position to optimize their educational dreams. If the reason for these obstacles disfavours certain ethnically or economically disadvantaged groups, then any notion of equalized university access will become nothing more than a boulevard of educational dreams.

References

Aboud, Frances E.
1981 "Ethnic Self-Identity." In R. Gardner and R. Kallin (eds) A Canadian Social Psychology of Ethnic Relations. Toronto: Methuen Publishers.

Acock, Alan C.
1985 "Parents and Their Children: The Study of Intergenerational Influence." Sociology and Social Research. Vol. 68 No. 2:151-171.

Ahamad, Bill
1987 Participation of Different Ethnic Groups in Postsecondary Education. Multiculturalism, Secretary of State.

Agnew, Robert S.
1983 "Social Class and Success Goals: An Examination of Relative and Absolute Aspirations." The Sociolgoical Quarterly. Vol. 24:435-452.

Akoodie, Mohhamad Ally
1984 "Identity and Self Concept in Immigrant Children." In R.J. Samuda, J.W. Berry and M. Lafferiere (eds) Multiculturalism in Canada: Social and Educational Perspectives. Toronto: Allyn and Bacon.

Allen, Walter R.
1980 "Preludes to Attainment: Race, Sex and Student Achievement Orientations." The Sociological Quarterly. Vol. 21:65-79.

Alwin, Duane F. and Arland Thorton
1984 "Family Origins and the Schooling Process: Early Versus Late Influence of Parental Characteristics." American Sociological Review. Vol. 49:784-802.

Alexander, Karl and Bruce K. Eckland
1975 "Contextual Effects in the High School Attainment Process." American Sociological Review. Vol. 40:402-416.

Alexander, Karl, L.; Edward D. McDill; James Fenness;y and Ronald J. D'Amico
1979 "School SES Influences-Composition or Context?", Sociology of Education. Vol. 52:222-237.

Anisef, Paul
1975 The Critical Juncture: Realization of the Educaitonal and Career Intentions of Grade 12 Students in Ontario. Toronto: Ministry of Colleges and Universities.

Anisef, Paul
1975b "Consequences of Ethnicity for Educational Plans Among Grade 12 Students." In A. Wolfgang (ed) Education of Immigrant Children. Toronto: Ontario Institute for Studies in Education.

Anisef, Paul; Marie-Andre Bertrand; Ulrike Hortian and Carl E. James
1985 Accessability to Postsecondary Education in Canada: A Review of Literature. Published by the Education Support Sector: Department of the Secretary of the state.

Anisef, Paul; Norman Okihiro and Carl E. James
1982 Losers and Winners. Toronto: Butterworth.

Anisef, Paul; Gottfired J. Paasche and Anthony Turrittin
1980 Is the Die Cast? Educational Achievement and Work Destinations of Ontario Youth. Toronto: Ministry of Colleges and Universities.

Baker, Holland Mary
1981 "Mother's Occupation and Children's Attainments." Pacific Sociological Review. Vol. .24:237-254.

Baks, Ishmael
1985 "Student Background, Educational Perceptions and Occupational Expectations in Trinidad." Canadian and International Education. Vol. 14:12-27.

Baker, David P. and Doris R. Entwisle
1987 "The Influence of Mothers on the Academic Expectations of Young Children: A Longitudinal Study of How Gender Differences Arise." Social Forces. Vol. 65:670-694.

Baletic, Zvonimir
1982 "International Migration and Econmic Development: With Special Reference to Yugoslavia." International Migration Review. Vol. 16:736-756.

REFERENCES

Banton, Michael
1966 "Race as a Social Category." Race. Vol. 8; No. 1:1-17.

Baum, Sandra R. and Saul Schwartz
1985 "Equity, Envy and Higher Education." Social Science Quarterly: 491-503.

Bennett, William S. and Noel P. Gist
1964 "Class and Family Influences on Student Aspirations." Social Forces. Vol. 43:167-173.

Bickell, Robert
1987 "Achievement and Ascription: A Comparison of Public and Private High Schools." Youth and Society. Vol. 18:99-126.

Blishen, Bernard; William Carrol and Cathering Moore
1987 "The 1981 Socioeconomic Index for Occupations in Canada." Canadian Review of Sociology and Anthropology." 24(4):465-488.

Blishen, Bernard and Hugh McRoberts
1976 "A Revised Socioeconomic Index for Occuapations in Canada." Canadian Review of Sociology and Anthropology. Vol. 13:71-79.

Berman, Gerals S. and Marie R. Haug
1975 Occupational and Educational Goals and Expectations: The Effects of Race and Sex." Social Problems. Vol. 23:166-181,

Bodnar, John
1975 "Materialism and Morality: Slavic-American Immigrants and Education, 1890-1940." Journal of Ethnic Studies. Vol. 3:1-19.

Breton, Raymond
1970 "Academic Stratification in Secondary Schools and the Educational Plans of Students." Canadian Review of Sociology and Anthropology. Vol. 7:17-34.

Breton R. and H. Roseborough
1971 "Ethnic Differences in Status." in Blishen, B. et al. (eds): Toronto: Mcmillan of Canada Ltd.

Brewer, Richard I. and Mary N. Haslum
1986 "Ethnicity: The Experience of Socio-Economic Disadvantage and Educational Attainment." British Journal of Education. Vol. 7:19-23.

Vrookover, W.B.; E.L. Ericson and L.M. Joiner
1967 "Educational Aspirations and Educational Plans in Relation To Academic Achievement and Socio-Economic Status." The School Review. Vol. 75:392-400.

Bullivant, Brian M.
1986 "Power and Control in the Multi-Ethnic School: Towards a Conceptual Model." Ethnic and Racial Studies. Vol. 5:52-70.

Buric, Olivera and Andjelka Zecevic
1967 "Social Networks in Yugoslavia." Journal of Marriage and the Family: 331-337.

Calliste, Agnes M.
1980 "Educational and Occupational Expectations of High School Students: The Effects of Socioeconomic Background, Ethnicity and Sex." Unpublished PhD Dissertation. Ontario Institute for Studies in Education.

Cameron, M. David
1987 "The Framework for Managing and Financing Post Secondary Educaiton in Canada." The Forum Papers, Halifax: The Institute for Research on Public Policy.

Canadian Family Tree
1967 "Prepared by the Canadian Citizenship Branch. Dept. of Manpower and Immigration, Ottawa.
1986 Census of Canada; Data collected from 20 per cent Sample Households 1988 Summary Tabulations of Language, Birth, Citizenship, Immigration, Income, Household and Dwelling Characteristics. Statistics Canada.

Clark, E; D. Cook and G. Fallis
1975 "Socialization, Family Background and the Secondary School System." Pyke, R. and E. Zureik (eds) Socilization and Values in Canadian Society. Toronto: McClellenad and Stewart Ltd.

Cohen, Elizabeth G.
1965 "Parental Factors in Educational Ability." Sociolgoy of Education: 405-425.

Cohen, Jere
1983 "Peer Influence on College Aspirations With Initial Aspirations Controlled." American Sociological Review. Vol. 48:728-734.

Cohen, Yinon and Andrea Tyree
1987 "Escape From Poverty: Determinants of Intergenerational Mobiltiy of Sons and Daughters of the Poor." Social Science Quarterly: 803-813.

Coleman, J.
1961 The Adolescent Society. Nesw York: Free Press.

Chrysdale, Stewart
1974 "Aspirations and Expectations of High School Youth." International Journal of Comparative Sociology. Vol 16:19-36.

Clifton, Rodney A.
1982 "Ethnic Differences in Academic Achievement Process in Canada." Social Science Research. Vol. 11:67-87.

Clifton, Rodney A.; Raymond A. Perry; Karen Parsonson and Stella Hryniuk.
1986 "Effects of Ethnicity and Sex on Teachers' Expectations of Junior High School Students." Sociology of Education. Vol. 59:58-67.

REFERENCES

Collins, Randal
1971 "Functional and Conflict Theories of Educational Stratification." American Sociological Review. Vol. 36:1002-1019.

Cummins, Jim
1986 "Empowering Minority Students: A Framework for Intervention." Harvard Educational Review. Vol. 56:18-35.

Cuneo, Carl J. and James E. Curtis
1975 "Social Ascription in the Educaitonal and Occupational Status Attainment of Urban Canadians." Canadian Review of Sociology and Anthropology. Vol. 12:6-24.

Danziger, Kurt
1978 "Differences in Acculturation and Patterns of Socialization Among Italian Immigrant Families." in E. Zureik and R.M. Pike (eds) Socialization and Social Values in Canadian Society, Vol. 2. Toronto: McClelland and Stewart Ltd.

Denis, A.B.
1979 "Educational Aspirations of Montreal Post-Secondary Students: Ethnic, Sex and Social Class Differences." In Elliott, J. (ed) Two Nations Many Cultures: Ethnic Groups in Canada. Toronto: Prentice Hall of Canada Ltd.

Deosoran, R.
1975 "Social Class, Self-Concept and Educational Expectations: A Social Psychological Study." PhD Dissertation. Toronto: University of Toronto.
1975 "Educaitonal Aspirations: What Matters? A Literature Review. Toronto Board of Educaiton for the City of Toronto.

DiMaggio, Paul and John Mohr
1985 "Cultural Capital, Educational Attainment, and Marital Selection." American Journal of Sociology. Vol. 90:1231-1261.

Dole, Arthur
1973 "Aspirations of Blacks and Whites for Their Children." Vocational Guidance Quarterly. Vol. 22:24-32.

Duncan, Beverly and Otis Dudley Duncan
1968 "Minorities and the Process of Stratification." American Sociological Review: 356-364.

Education in Canada
1987 A Statistical Reveiw for 1985-86. Statistics Canada Ministry of Supply and Services Canada.

Elder, Glen H.
1965 "Family Structure and Educational Attainment: A Cross-National Analysis." American Sociological Review: 81-96.

Empey, LaMar T.

1956 Social Class and Occupational Aspirations: A Comparison of Absolute and Relative Measurement." American Sociolgical Review. Vol. 21:703-709.

Entwisle, D. and L. Hayduk

1981 "Academic and Expectations and the School Attainment of Young Children." Sociology of Education. Vol. 54:34-50.

Eterovich, F. and A. Spalatin

1970 Croatia: Land People and Culture. Toronto: University of Toronto Press.

Featherman, David L.

1971 "The Socioeconomic Achievement of White Religio-Ethnic Subgroups: Social and Psychological Explanations." American Sociological Review. Vol. 36:207-222.

Fleming, W. 1974 Educaitonal Opportunity: The Pursuit of Equality. Toronto: Prentice Hall of Canada.

Forum Papers

1987 National Forum Secretariat Halifax: The Institute For Research on Public Policy.

Gadzella, Bernadette M and Glenn P. Fournet

1975 "Differences of High and Low Achievers on Self-Perceptions." Journal of Experimental Educaiotn. Vol. 44:44-48.

Garnier, Maurice A. and Lawrence E. Raffalovish

1984 "The Evolution of Equality of Educational Opporunities in France." Sociology of Education. Vol 57:1-11.

Gaskell, Jane and Marvin Lazerson

1981 "Between School and Work: Perspectives of Working Class Youth." Interchange. Vol. 11:80-96.

Gilbert, Syd and Hugh a MCRoberts

1977 "Academic Stratification and Education Plans: A Reassessmetn." Canadian Review of Sociology and Anthropology. Vol.. 14:34-47.

Globe and Mail

1986 "That Certain Degree of Distinction." Sept. 10.

1987 "Flag-Raising is Insult." April, 28.

1987 "Classes Saddling Minority Children With 'label for life', Teachers told." Nov. 13.

Grabb, Edward G.

1987 "Social Stratification." In James J. teewan (ed.) Sociology: A Canadian Introduction. Scarborough: Prentice-Hall Canada Inc.

Guppy, Neil

1984 "Access to Higher Education in Canada." Canadian Journal of Higher Educaiton. Vol. 14:79-93.

REFERENCES

Guppy, Neil; Paulina D. Mikicich and Ravi Pendakur
1984 "Changing Patterns of Educational Inequality in Canada." Canadian Journal fo Sociology. Vol 9:319-331.

Haller, Archibald O.
1968 "On the Concept of Aspiration." Rural Sociolgoy. Vol. 33:484-487.

Harvey, Edward B.
1984 "The Changing Relationship Between University Education and Intergenerational Social Mobility." Canadian Review of Sociolgoy and Anthropology. Vol. 21:275-286.

Herman, Harry V.
1979 "Ethnic Diversity and Conflict in Canada." Paper presented at The Annual Meeting of the Canadian Sociology and Anthropology Conference, Saskatoon, Saskatchewan, Canada.

1978 "Ethnicity and Occupation: Comparative Analysis of the Occupational Choices of Croatian and Macedonian Immigrants of Ontario." PhD Dissertation. Toronto: University of Toronto.

Heyneman, Stephen P.
1976 "Influences on Academic Achievement: Comparison of Results from Uganda and More Industrialised Societies." Sociology of Education. Vol. 49:200-211.

Higginbotham, Elizabeth
1985 "Race and Class Barriers to Black Women's College Attendance." Journal of Ethnic Studies." Vol. 13:89-107.

Hirschmann, Charles and Morrison G. Wong
1984 "Socioeconomic Gains of Asian Americans, Blacks and Hispanics: 1960-1976." American Journal of Sociology. Vol. 90:584-607.

HOljevac, V.
1967 Hrvati Izvan Domovine (Croatians Outside Their Homeland) Zagreb, Groatia, Yugoslavia: Matica Hrvatska.

Howell, Frank and Wolfgang Frese
1979 "Race, Sex, and Aspirations: Evidence for the 'Race' Convergence Hypothesis." Sociology of Educaiton. Vol. 52:34-46.

Husen, T.
1974 Talent, Equality and Meritocracy. The Hague, Maritimus Nyhoff.

Inbar, Michael
1977 "Immigration and Learning: The Vulnerable Age." Candian Review of Sociology and Anthropology. Vol. 14:218-234.

Inbar, Michael and Chaim Adler
1976 "The Vulnerable Age: Serendipitous FIndings." Sociology of Educaiton. Vo. 49:193-200.

Jacobs, Jerry A.
1987 "The Sex of Aspirations and Occupations: Instability During the Careers of Young Women." Social Sciecne Quarterly:122-137.

James, Karl
1980 "Peer Influence on Educational and Occupational Aspirations and Achievement." M.A. Thesis. Toronto: York University.
1986 "The Challenge of Making It: Youth's Career Aspirations and Perceptions of Their Chances to Achieve." PhD Dissertation. Toronto: York Univeristy.

Jansen, Clifford
1981 Education and Social Mobility of Immigrants: A Pilot Study Foccusingt on Italians in Vancouver. Toronto: York University I.B.R.

Jencks, Christopher
1972 Inequality: A Reassessment of the Effects of Family and Schooling in America. New York: Basic BOoks Inc.

Jensen, F. Gary
1986 "Explaining Differences in Academic Behaviour Between Public-School and Catholic-School Students: A Quantitative Case Study." Sociology of Education. Vol. 59:32-41.

Jones, Frank E.
1981 "Age at Immigration and Educaitonal Attainment." Canadian Review of Sociology and Anthropology. Vol. 18:393-405.

Kahl, Joseph H.
1953 "Educational adn Occupational Aspirations of "Common Man" Boys." Harvard Educational Review. Vol. 23:186-203.

Kandel, Denise B.
1969 "parental adn Peer Influences on Educational Plans of Adolescents." American Sociological Review. Vol. 34:213-223.

Karlovic, N.L.
1982 "Internal Colonialism in a Marxist Society: The Case of Croatia." Ethnic and Racial Studies. Vol. 5:277-299.

Kasinski, L.
1978 "Yugoslavia and International Migration." Canadian Slovanic Papers. Vol. 20:314-338.

Kerckhoff, Alan C. and Richard T. Campbell
1977 "Race and Social Differences in the Explanation of Educational Ambition." Social Forces. Vol. 55:701-714.

King, A.J.C.
1968 "Ethnicity and School Adjustment." Canadian Review of Sociology and Anthropolgoy. Vol. 5:81-91.

REFERENCES

Kifer, Edward
1975 "Relationship Bewteen AScademic Achievement and Personality Characteristics: A Quasi Longitudinal Study." Amercian Educational Research Journal. Vol. 12:191-210.

Krauss, I.
1964 "Sources of Educational Aspirations Among Working Class Youth." American Sociological review. Vol. 29:867-879.

Krauze, Tadeusz and Kazimierz M. Slomczynski
1985 "How Far to Meritocracy? Empirical Tests of Controversial Thesis." Social Forces. VOl. 63:623-642.

Kromkowski, John A.
1986 "Eastern and Southern European Immigrants: Expectations, Reality, and a New Agenda." Annals, AAPSS, 487: 57-77.

Lareau, Annette.
1987 "Social Class Differences in Family-School Relationships: The Importance of Cultural Capital." Sociology of Educaiton. Vol. 60:73-85.

Li, Peter S.
1988 Ethnic Inequality: In a Class Society. Toronto: Wall and Thompson.
1978 "The Stratification of Ethnic Immigrants: The Case of Toronto." Canadian Review of Sociology and Anthropology. Vol. 15:41-49.

Lieberson, Stanley and Mary Waters
1986 "Ethnic Groups in Flux: The Changing Ethnic Responses of American Whites." Annals, AAPSS, 487-79-91.

Mare, Robert D.
1981 "Change and Stability in Educational Stratification." American Sociological Review Vol. 46:72-87.

Martell, G.
1974 The Politics of Canadian Public Schools. Toronto: Lorimer Publishers.

Marjoribanks, Kevin
1978 "Ethnicity, Family Environment and Cognitive Performance." Psychological Reports. Vol. 42:1277-1278.
1980 "Ethclass, the Achievement Syndrome and Children's Cognitive Performance." The Journal of Educational Reserach: 327-333.

Maxwell Mary Percival and James D. Maxwell
1984 "Women and the Elite: Educational and Occupational Aspirations of Private School Females 1966/1976." Canadian Review of Sociolgoy and Anthropology. Vol. 21:371-394.

Maykovich, Minako K.
1975 "Ethnic Variation in Success Value." in Pike R. and R. Zureik (eds) Socialization and Values in Canadian Society. Toronto: McClelland and Stewart.

Mueller, Charles W.
1980. "Evidence on the Relationship Between Religion and Educational Attainment." Sociology of Education. Vol. 53:140-152.

Murphy, Raymond
1977 "Societal Values and Reaction of Teachers to Students' Backgrounds." Canadian Review of Sociology and Anthropology. Vol. 14:48-56.

Nelson, B.
1970 Sociological Perspectives in Education. Toronto: Pitman Publishers.

Nelson, Joel I.
1972 "High School Context and College Plans: The Impact of Social Structure on Aspirations." American Sociological Review. Vol. 37:143-148.

Oakes, Jeannie.
1983 "Limiting Opportunity: AStudent Race and Curricular Differences in Secondary Vocational Education." American Journal of Sociolgoy. Vol. 91:328-355.
1986 "Tracking, Inequality, and the Rhetoric of Reform: Why Schools Don't Change." Journal of Educaiton. Vol. 168:60-80.

Organization for Economic Co-Operation and Development
1976 Reviews of National Policies for Education: Canada
1981 Reveiw of National Policies for Educaiton: Yugoslavia.
1970 Innovations in Higher Education: Reforms in Yugoslavia.

Otto, Luther B.
1977 "Girl Friends as Significant-Others: Their Influence on Young Men's Career Aspirations and Achievements." Sociometry. Vol. 40:287-293.

Otto, Luther B. adn Archibald O. Haller
1977 "Evidence for a Social Psycholoical View of the Status Attinament Process: Four Studies COmpared." Social Forces. Vol. 57:887-914.

Padget, D.
1980 "Symbolic Ethnicity and Patterns of Ethnic Identity Assertion of American Born Serbs." Ethnic Groups. Bol. 3:55-77.

Pascarella, Ernest T.
1984 "College Environmetnal Influences on Students' Educational Aspirations." Journal of Higher Education. Vol. 55:751-771.

Paveskovic, Nedo
1970 "Croatians in Canada." in Eterovich, F. and C. Spalatin (eds) Croatia: Land, People, Cutlure. Toronto U of T. Press.

Picou, Steven J. and T. Michael Carter
1976 "Significant-Others Influence and Aspirations." Sociology of Educaiton. Vol. 49:12-22.

REFERENCES

Pike, S.
1977 Sex Role Socialization in the School System." in Carleton, R.; L. Colley and N. MacKinnon (eds) Educaitonal Change and Society: A Sociology of Canadian Education. Toronto: Gage Publishers.

Plewis, Ian
1987 "Social Disadvantage, Educational Attainment and Ethnicity: A Commetn." British Journal of Sociology of Education. Vol. 8:77-82.

Porter, John
1965. The Vertical Mosaic: An Analysis of Social Class and Power in Canada. Toronto: U. of T. Press.

1976 "Socialization and Mobiltiy in Educational and Early Occupational Attainment." Sociology of Education. Vol. 46:23-33.

1979 The Measure of Canadian Soceity: Education, Equality and Opportunity. Toronto: Gage Publishers.

Porter, John; Marion Porter adn Bernard Blishen
1973 Does Money Matter: Prospects for Higher Education in Ontario. Toronto: York University, I.B.R.

Porter, John; Marion Porter and Bernard Blishen
1982 Stations and Callings: Making Through the School System. Toronto: Methuen.

Portes, Alejandro
1984 "The Rise of Ethnicity: Determinants of Ethnci Perceptions Among Cuban Exiles in Miami." American Sociological Review. Vol. 49:383-397.

Radecky, H. 1979 Ethnic Organizational Dynamics: The Polish Group in Canada. Waterloo: Wilfrid Laurier University Press.

Rasporich, Anthony W.
1979 For a Better Life. Manuscript.
1982 For a Better Life: A History of Croatians in Canada. Toronto: McClelland and Stewart Limited.

Rehrberg, Richard A. and David L. Westby
1967 "Parental Encouragement, Occuapation, Education and Family Size: Artifactual or Independent Determinants of Adolescent Educational Aspirations." Social Forces: 362-374.

Reitzes, Donald C. and Elizabeth Mutran
1980 "Significant Others and Self-Conceptions: Influencing Educational Expectations and Academic Performance." Sociology of Education. Vol. 53:21-32.

Rex, John
1973 Race, Colonialism and the City. London: Routledge and Kegan, Paul Ltd.

Richmond, Anthony
1986 "Ethnogenerational Variabion in Educational Achievement." York University.

Richmond, A.H; and W.E. Kalbach
1980 Factors in the Adjustment of Immigrants and Their Descendants. Ottawa: Ministry of Supply and Demand.

Rodman, Hyman
1967 "Marital Power in France, Greece, Yugoslavia and the United States: A Cross-National Discussion," Journal of the Marriage and the Family: 321-339.

Rogler, Lloyd h.; Rosemary Santana Cooney and Vilma Ortiz
1980 "Intergenerational Change in Ethnic Identity in the Puerto Rican Family." International Migration Review. Vol. 13:193-214.

Rompkey, Bill
1986 "Canada's Need For a National Strategy for Postsecondary Educatoin." The Canadian Journal of Higher Education. Vol. xvi-3:1-6.

Rosen, Bernard
1959 "Race, Ethnicity and the Achievement Syndrome." American Sociological Review. Vol. 24:47-61.

Rudd, Ernest
1984 "Whose Children go to University." Higher Educational Review: 27-38.

Ryder, N.B.
1955 "The Interpretation of Origin Statistics." Canadian Journal of Economy and Political Science. Vol. 34:466-479.

Sacks, Maurie
1985 "Without Tradition You are Blak: Ethnic Heritage Education in American Today." Ethnic Groups. Vol. 6:249-273.

Sandis, Eva E.
1970 "The Transmission of Mother's Educational Ambitions, as Related to Specific Socialization Techniques." Journal of the Marriage and the Family. Vol. 32:32-40.

Satzewich, Victor and Peter S. Li
1987 "Immigrant Labour in Canada: The Cost and Benefit of Ethnic ORigin in the Job Market." Canadian Journal of Sociology 12(3):229-241.

Shapiro, Bernard J.
1986 "The Public Fuding of Private Schools in Ontario: The Setting, Some Arguments, and Some Matters of Belief." Vol. 11:264-277.

Shavit, Yossi
1984 "Tracking and Ethnicity in Israeli Secondary Schools." American Sociological Review. Vol. 49:210-220.

REFERENCES

Shamai, Shmuel and Philip R.D. Corrigan
1987 "Social Facts, Moral Regulation and Statistical Juridiction: A Critical Evaluation of Candaidn Census Figures on Education." The Canadian Journal of Higher Education. Vol. xvii-2:37-58.

Sewell, William H.; Archibald O. Haller and Alejandro Portes
1969 "The Educational and Early Occupational Attainment Process." American Sociolgoical Review. Vol. 34:82-91.

Sewell, William H. and Vimal P. Shah
1968 "Parents' Education and Children's Educational Aspirations and Achievements." American Sociological Reveiw. Vol. 33:191-209.

Stafford, Kathy L.; Sven B. Lundstedt adn Arthur D. Lynn
1984 "Social and Economic Factors Affecting Participation in Higher Educaiton." Journal of Higher Education. Vol. 55:590-608.

Stryker, Robyn
1981 "Religio-Ethnic Effects on Attainments in the Early Career." American Sociolgoical Review. Vol. 46:212-231.

Teachman, D.Jay
1987 "Family Background, Educational Resources, and Educational Attainment." American Sociolgoical Review. Vol. 52:548-557.

Temple, Mark and Kenneth Polk
1986 "A Dynamic Analysis of Educational Attainment." Sociolgoy of Education. Vol. 59:79-84.

Tomovic, V.
1979 Definitions in Sociology: Covergence, Confloict, and Alternative Vocabularies. St. Catherines: Diliton Publications Inc.

Toronto Daily Star
1980 "Education Theory Worth Test." Jan. 18.
1980 "A Flag Undeserving of Honour." April 19.
1984 "Schools Discourage Portuguese Students Parents' Goup Says." Nov. 28.
1985 "Blacks Being Pushed Aside Teacher Says." may 1.
1985 "Metro: A Model of Multiculturalism." Dec. 26.
1986 "Won't Single Out Black Students for Racism Stuidy, Officials Wow." OCt. 16.
1987 "Portuguese-Born Woman is Author of a New Math Text." March 2.

Trent, William W.
1984 "Equaltiy Considerations in Higher Education: race and Sex Differences in Degree Attainment and Major Field from 1976 thorugh 1981." American Journal of Education. Voll. 92:281-305.

Trovato, Frank and Carl F. Grindstaff
1986 "Economic Status: A Census Analysis of Thirty Year Old Immigrant Women in Canada. VOl. 23:568-587.

Wood, Dean
1981 "School in a Multi-Ethnic Society: Responding to Prejudice and Discrimination", Canadian Ethnic Studies. Vol. 17:125-129.

Wechsler, Harold S.
1984 "The Rationale for Restriction: Ethnicity and College Admissions in America, 1910-1980." American Quarterly. Vol. 36: 643-667.

Williams, Jenny
1986 "Education and Race: The Racialisation of Class Inequalities." British Journal of Sociology of Education. Vol. 7: 135-154.

Williams, Trevor H.
1972 "Educational Aspirations: Longitudinal Evidence on Their Development in Candian Youth." Sociology of Education." Vol. 45: 107-133.

Wilson, Kenneth L. and Alajandro Portes
1975 The Educational Attainment Process: Results From a National Sample." American Journal of Sociology. Vol. 81: 343-363.

Wood, Dean
1983 "Schools in a Multi-Ethnic Society: Responding to Prejudice and Discrimination." Canadian Ethnic Studies, XV, 2:125-129.

Yancey, William; Eugene P. Ericksen and Richard N. Julianai
1976 "Emergent Ethnicity: A Review and Reformulation." American Sociological Review. Vol. 41:391-403.